SUSTAINING POWERS

Love,

[signature]

C A T H Y   P O W E R S

ISBN 978-1-931117-71-5

9 781931 117715

Item: SPRG

Published by Lash & Associates Publishing/Training Inc.
100 Boardwalk Drive, Suite 150, Youngsville, NC 27596
Tel: (919) 556-0300

This book is part of a series on brain injury among children, adolescents, adults and veterans.
For a free catalog, contact Lash & Associates
Tel: (919) 556-0300 or visit our web site www.lapublishing.com

LASH & ASSOCIATES PUBLISHING/TRAINING INC.

100 BOARDWALK DRIVE, SUITE 150, YOUNGSVILLE, NC 27596
TEL: (919) 556-0300 FAX: (919) 556-0900

WWW.LAPUBLISHING.COM

DEDICATED

From the deepest parts

of my heart and soul

to my beautiful son

Bryce Kenneth Powers

I love you forever!

Momma

TABLE OF CONTENTS

FOREWORD

There are over 2.5 million people in the United States of America who suffer from traumatic brain injury (TBI) every year. Of that vast number, more than 280,000 individuals are admitted to a hospital due to TBI. Moderate and severe brain injury causes significant physical and cognitive deficits that require intensive care early in management and extensive rehabilitation. A subset of persons with severe TBI suffers from a prolonged disorder of consciousness. This is when a person is in a coma, vegetative state, or minimally responsive state. For these individuals, time is the best treatment. However, time takes its toll, not only on the person afflicted with TBI, but also on the family and support network for that person.

Sustaining Powers is an in-depth account of the trials the Powers family experienced after the severe injury of their son, Bryce. Throughout the experience, Cathy Powers displayed her ordeal on a social media platform for the world to read, support, and critique. However, at the same time, the fractured emotional state of an actively grieving mother did not allow her to unyieldingly paint those emotions for all to read on social media. It is only in this book that she breaks down her wall and candidly shares her thoughts and emotions. Through a strong faith in God and devotion to her child, Cathy demonstrates a resilience that allows her to survive this experience.

As such, Cathy's experience provides caregivers and families an understanding of the long and rough road that many people must take to help their loved one improve or let go. Although this book is about the experience after TBI, it can be easily translated to any recovery after a traumatic accident or severe illness. The book describes the cognitive and physical issues that happen to a patient, but also the psychological and spiritual injuries that occur to families. Never does a severe injury or illness affect only one person, but rather a whole family unit. Often, medical professionals are unaware of the full struggles of families or caregivers, so this book will give those professionals a better understanding of families' needs.

I have known the Powers family for over four years. My relationship with them started as a physician who could give them hope, but changed over time into a caring friend. In the five months that Bryce was at the Hunter Holmes McGuire VA Medical Center in Richmond, Virginia, I only experienced a small glimpse into the emotions of a grieving parent. Only through this book am I able to truly understand the grief Cathy experienced as she moved between the strain of hope for recovery of a severely injured child to the grief of understanding the loss and letting go.

Ajit B Pai, MD
Chief, Physical Medicine & Rehabilitation
Hunter Holmes McGuire VA Medical Center
Richmond, Virginia

AUTHOR'S NOTE

This book is a description of my journey from the first moments I learned of my son's life-changing auto accident. It has been written using a combination of portions of the public Facebook updates that I made during the actual events as they happened, combined with my vulnerable thoughts, memories, and behind-the-scenes information, which I call "Life Offline." I hope that together these will allow an even deeper glimpse into our "new normal" life. My prayer is that as I share the peaks and valleys of our family's experience, somehow with God's help, your faith will be made stronger.

Love, Cathy

PROLOGUE

On Saturday, October 13, 2012, Airman Bryce Powers woke up mid-morning on his base in Misawa, Japan, 400 miles north of Tokyo. He had worked hard all week in the Air Force Munitions "bomb dump," and it was finally his day off. He made a cup of pumpkin spice coffee with his Keurig machine and checked his emails. When his hunger reached its peak, he went to the chow hall for a meal. That's where he ran into three of his Aircraft Munitions Maintenance Organization (AMMO) coworkers.

At some point, discussions of a day trip to Lake Towada began. Lake Towada is the largest crater lake on the island of Honshu and the twelfth largest lake in Japan. It is well known for its beautiful scenery and clear water. It's a favorite spot for local troops since it's only a forty-five minute drive from base.

Four airmen decided to go, taking two cars. Bryce drove his Suzuki Cappuccino, powered by a motorcycle engine, taking one passenger with him, and the other two took a second car. Bryce was unfamiliar with the roads and unsure of the route to the lake. The other driver knew the way and offered to take the lead, so Bryce agreed to follow behind.

After finishing their meal and getting cleaned up, the four airmen met at the base shoppette. They purchased an array of drinks and snacks to take with them to Lake Towada. The excited airmen got into the two cars, and with smiles on their faces, their impromptu day trip began.

The two cars exited the base, turned right at the train station, and went approximately one and a half miles down Route 22. They went up a little hill where the road was winding and forested, and at the top they turned to the right. The roads were clear, and the sun was shining. It was a beautiful fall afternoon.

The driver of the lead car said he looked back and Bryce wasn't behind him anymore, so he slowed and waited for him to catch up. When he didn't come around the curve for several minutes, the airman turned around, drove back and found Bryce's wrecked two-seat convertible on the side of the road resting against a large concrete pole.

The two airmen quickly exited their vehicle and ran to investigate the accident scene. They found Bryce unconscious and his passenger bleeding and moaning. The door had crimped in on their AMMO sister, causing internal injuries. The twisted metal and rubber steering wheel was no longer round. Bryce's side of the car was partially up in the air, and the left side was wedged into the muddy terrain.

They unbuckled Bryce and tried lifting him, but because of the angle of the car, he was too heavy. They went to the other side, unbuckled the passenger, carried her across the road, and laid her in a field. Then they came back and were able to pull Bryce from the car and call for help.

Bryce never woke up. His AMMO brothers said that when they laid him in the field, he was making gurgling noises and vomiting.

Both American and Japanese medics were dispatched to the scene, where first aid was administered. Unconscious and aspirating on the blood filling his lungs, Bryce was loaded into a Japanese transport vehicle.

There is a simple outpatient clinic on base, so the Japanese medics drove him there. On the way, Bryce went into respiratory failure and stopped breathing. The medics didn't have training on intubation or even the supplies to bag him. When they arrived at the base, they had to take the time to go through the security checkpoint, and all the while Bryce was without oxygen.

When they finally arrived at the clinic, the base maxillofacial dental surgeon attempted to intubate Bryce. The first attempt failed, so he tried again. But when they checked with a stethoscope, no air was moving through his lungs. So he pulled all the tubing out and began a third attempt. At this point, they could finally hear oxygen moving into one side of his lungs.

Each intubation procedure took approximately two minutes to complete, which left Bryce without the optimum level of oxygen to his brain for more than six minutes.

Due to the critical nature of Bryce's injuries, he was packed into an ambulance and the military medics drove him to the regional Japanese trauma hospital in Hachinohe. It was a one-hour drive.

Chapter One

Early Morning Phone Call

I awoke to the sound of our home phone ringing early on a Saturday morning. It was October 13, 2012. I've never been much of a morning person, but I instantly threw back the covers, jumped out of bed, and ran to the phone. I knew it had to be my twenty-year-old son, Bryce, calling from overseas.

He was literally on the other side of the world—exactly a half day ahead of me. When he deployed to Asia, I learned that noon for me was midnight for Bryce. Every call he made home meant the world to me, and I was always excited to hear his voice. Most often he would call when I was already awake. But sometimes, with his busy military schedule, he called at odd hours. I didn't mind, and he knew it! But he also knew that he was the only one who could get away with waking me up so early in the morning. It is no secret in our house that this redheaded Irish Momma has never been a morning person.

I grabbed the receiver and said, "Hello," but was caught off guard when I didn't hear Bryce's voice. Instead, there was a woman on the other end of the line.

"Hello, this is Lieutenant Colonel Karen Branch, Bryce's Commanding Officer in Misawa. Are you the mother of Bryce Powers?"

"Yes," I answered with a tone of weary confusion.

"There has been an accident…"

Immediately I started freaking out.

Her words were serious and official, yet at the same time her voice was filled with care and compassion. "Bryce is in critical condition. The accident happened off base, and the doctors are not sure if he is going to make it. He's been taken to a hospital here in Japan."

In an instant time seemed to stop as I realized something traumatic had happened to Bryce. My mind was suddenly in a fog.

I stood at the foot of my bed intermittently hearing only parts of her sentences: "Bryce was driving off base" … "passenger in the car with him" … "terrible accident" … "in a coma" … "ventilators" … "critical condition…"

Then she said the most devastating thing: "We're not sure he will make it through the night."

At first I was trying to determine if this was actually reality! In the movies, when something bad happens to your child in the military, someone in uniform knocks on your door. But this was a phone call from a stranger explaining Bryce might not live through the night… how could this be real?

Once I verified that this really was Bryce's Lieutenant Colonel on the phone, I instantly went in to a state of shock. I began asking "parent's worst nightmare" type questions, which woke my husband, Jim. "It's the Air Force. Something bad happened to Bryce."

The panicked tone in my voice caused Jim to jump out of bed and switch our phone to speaker mode. Instantly wide awake, he asked what had happened. The Air Force officer started from the beginning, retelling the horrific news.

I looked at Jim, watching as he intently listened to her every word. He spoke the occasional, "Yes, ma'am," in between her sentences, as he calmly and completely took control of the situation. Moments before he had been sound asleep and now here he was at the foot of our bed in his underwear, completely calm as he stood with perfect upright posture. He had instantly transformed into a tough American soldier receiving an intelligence report along with his unit's battle plans.

Wow! At that moment I appreciated my Air Force veteran husband's military background more than I ever had before. I knew he had this, so I crumbled. The next thing I remember, I was running through our house screaming to wake our sixteen-year-old daughter, Madison.

If I had it to do over again, I would have entered her bedroom and sat down beside her, lovingly stroking her hair and allowing her to peacefully wake up. Then I would have calmly explained the news of the accident and Bryce's medical condition, hugging her tightly. I'd have reassured her that God is one hundred percent in control, and that He was with Bryce in Japan! Then we would have prayed for Bryce's healing together.

Unfortunately, you don't always get a second chance to do things right. I ran in to Madison's room in a complete panic, screaming and crying. My screams instantly jolted her wide awake. I will always remember the terror and fear that filled her eyes. Before I could even explain what had happened to Bryce, Madison was screaming and crying as loudly as I was.

In that moment I snapped, too broken to realize the heavy toll of emotional damage I was heaping onto my sweet, sensitive daughter. I just kept screaming and yelling out the bit of information I remembered from the phone call.

"Bryce was in a horrible accident in Japan! He's in a coma! He's on a ventilator! He probably won't live through the night!" Months later, Madison shared that this was the one experience that haunted her the most.

When I got back to our room, Jim was still on the phone with the military taking care of emergency travel plans.

The next couple of hours were a blur for me. As I left Madison's room, Jim told me exactly what needed to be done. "The Air Force said they're going to get you a ticket to fly out of Charlotte this afternoon. So you need to take a shower and get packed. We need to get this done as soon as possible because we don't know when the flight will be."

None of this information was registering with me. I remember Jim telling me, "You've got to do this, and you've got to do that," and I'd say, "Okay," and then I would run outside for no apparent reason. Jim would follow after me saying, "You need to get in here and do this."

Still in shock, I frantically ran back and forth through our house, filled with fear and unable to stop crying. I felt like I should be doing something to help Bryce, but I knew there was nothing I could do until I got to him. All of a sudden, an idea hit me. I could pray for Bryce and ask others to pray for him too!

I turned on the computer and quickly set up a prayer page for Bryce on Facebook. I thought it would be a place where I could keep family and friends updated on his condition. It was also a desperate attempt to quickly find as many prayer warriors as I could for Bryce. I immediately posted an SOS message on Facebook saying that the military called and we need to pray for Bryce.

Facebook Update: Saturday 10/13/12, 7:00 a.m.

OMG! The Air Force just called. They are on the phone now! Bryce is in a coma! He is on a ventilator! OMG! Help!

Life Offline

I had no idea then that these Facebook updates would become a vital part of my daily life for months to come.

I was able to create the prayer page in just a couple of minutes. Honestly, it was a simple copy and paste job. The strange, yet amazing, thing was that the previous December I had created another prayer page to rally support for a dear friend, Stacy Skelly, whose son, Marine Corporal Tyler Skelly, was terribly injured in Bahrain. He was also in a coma and on a ventilator, having suffered a traumatic brain injury (TBI). Stacy had to leave her family, job, and home to fly to Germany to be with her son.

Stacy and I have been great friends since our sons were just little guys. What are the chances that something this bad could have happened to both our boys? I simply created and monitored Tyler's prayer and support page to help keep his family and friends updated and to get prayer warriors to pray for Tyler's healing. Never in my imagination did I think I would need a similar prayer and support page for my own son!

Facebook Update: Saturday 10/13/12, 10:16 a.m.

I, Cathy Powers, just created this page for our son. Please pray!

Life Offline

Jim saw me working on the computer, not knowing that I was setting up a prayer page, and he reminded me that I needed to get ready. I remember Jim grabbing me, putting his face right in front of my face and saying, "Listen, underwear … what underwear do you want? Tell me."

He would tell me what I needed to do, and I would say okay. Then he would leave and I would start doing something crazy. Then he would come back and say, "What toiletries do you need?" At one point, he held onto my shoulders and kind of shook me. Then he repeated the same lines, word for word.

It was decided fairly quickly I would be leaving for Japan alone. I was the only one in our family with a valid passport. I had applied for one as soon as Bryce learned that his first duty station overseas would be Osan, South Korea. I wasn't keen on the idea of flying over the ocean, but I got my passport anyway in case something ever happened to Bryce. I wanted to be able to get to him in case of an emergency.

I'm so thankful I did.

Madison wanted to go with me and had initially been told she could. She had packed her suitcase and was ready to go. One phone call later, the offer was rescinded due to her minor status and lack of a passport. The military casualty liaison said it would be impossible to get her an emergency passport in the couple of hours we had. She was crushed by the thought she might not ever see her big brother alive again.

I had a special two-foot by three-foot photo blanket of Bryce and me hugging that a friend of mine had specially ordered and sent to me after Bryce moved overseas. Madison took it upon herself to fold it and pack it inside my suitcase. When I arrived in Japan,

I found it in my luggage, and it brought me great comfort. The Hachinohe City Hospital intensive care unit (ICU) staff let me hang it on an IV pole near Bryce.

As soon as we finished packing, the Air Force called with the flight information. It was five minutes after 12, and we had less than an hour and a half to get to the airport.

Jim had a passport for years, loved to travel, and even spent his first five years in the Air Force overseas in Germany. Unfortunately, his passport had expired and then was stolen, so it was going to take a lot of time and paperwork to get a new one. Knowing it would slow me down and possibly keep me from Bryce's side, Jim decided it was best that he stay home. This would allow him to continue working to provide for our family while he took care of Madison, our home, and our pets. His number one goal was to get me overseas as soon as possible so Bryce would have his Momma with him.

As I waited to leave for the airport, I added another update to Bryce's Facebook prayer and support page. I knew he needed God's help right then more than anything else.

Facebook Update: Saturday 10/13/12, 12:10 p.m.

The Air Force just called. I leave for Japan today at 4:30 p.m.

The Air Force representative had worked quickly to find connecting flights from Charlotte, North Carolina, to Misawa, Japan.

Facebook Update: Saturday 10/13/12, 1:15 p.m.

I'm leaving for the airport now. I fly from Charlotte to Los Angeles, Los Angeles to Tokyo, and then Tokyo to Misawa. Air Force personnel will meet me at the Misawa airport. I'm not sure of any other details. I just want to be with Bryce, and to kiss his face. He is a Christian, and knows Jesus. I am scared, but will keep praying. Please pray!

Love, Cathy

When we arrived at the airport in Charlotte, all the paperwork was waiting for us and the tickets were at the counter. The authorities gave special permission for Jim and Madison to go through security and to stay in the USO with me before the flight.

Facebook Update: Saturday 10/13/12, 2:15 p.m.

I am sitting in the Charlotte airport USO with Bryce's Dad and Sister. This is the last place we spent with Bryce before he left for Japan. We are all stunned and scared.

Thank you so much for praying for Bryce!

Love, Cathy

As we sat in the USO, we discussed what I might find in Japan—whether or not Bryce would still be alive and what I would do if the doctors wanted me to take him off life support. Jim told me very clearly, "Do not make the decision of whether he lives or dies. I will do that for the family. Don't sign any papers."

I thought it was so weird that he said that to me before I left. Ultimately, I wanted God to make that decision.

Before I boarded the plane, I checked Bryce's prayer and support page and was so encouraged when I saw this message:

"Cathy - We are actively praying in Japan also. We've rallied support, to include the base chaplains. We're ready for you when you arrive. - Lieutenant Colonel Karen Branch, Bryce's Commanding Officer."

I had been worrying nonstop about Bryce and his condition, wondering if he was scared, hurting, and alone in the fight for his precious life. Seeing this friendly and loving message gave me hope that at least Bryce was surrounded by a supportive, compassionate, and praying military family. I took comfort in the thought that I would be there soon!

I don't remember the flight to Los Angeles, but I do remember being at Los Angeles International Airport (LAX). All of a sudden it dawned on me that I was in charge of myself now. I read a Facebook message on my phone from an Air Force mom, also known as a "wing sister," saying that she and her husband would meet me in the LAX USO.

So I located and checked into the USO, and inside the couple was waiting to greet me. They led me to a table and ordered something to drink.

After a few moments, the USO manager came over and said, "Excuse me, Cathy Powers? Someone with the Air Force in Japan is on the phone for you."

I picked up the phone and First Sergeant Faith Jackson introduced herself to me. She asked about my flight and how I was doing. She then gave me a quick update on Bryce, basically saying there were no changes in his health status. She told me that she had received more details about the accident, and apparently Bryce wasn't the driver after all; he was the passenger.

I remember being worried that Bryce was not only hurt, but that he was going to be in trouble if something happened to his passenger because he was driving. I felt a slight bit of relief when she told me the other AMMO person was driving.

Facebook Update: Saturday 10/13/12, 10:00 p.m.

I landed safely in Los Angeles and met up with two Air Force parents in the USO. I will leave for Tokyo around midnight (PST). The flight is twelve and one-half hours. Then, I will have a three-hour layover before boarding another plane to Misawa, Japan. Air Force personnel will meet me there, and bring me to Bryce's hospital. No changes to his condition as of yet. I love and appreciate each of you!

Thank you for loving our son, and praying for him.

Love, Cathy

Life Offline

As eager as I was to get to Bryce, I also struggled with my fear of flying. In my younger years, I loved to fly. As a matter of fact, I loved to skydive too! That adventurous spirit left in my thirties.

I will never forget the day I boarded a small prop plane for a business trip. I found my seat and was trying desperately to fasten my seat belt, which was not exactly overweight friendly. It was a struggle, but I finally won! Probably due to the extra exertion, I was hot and felt confined. It seemed like the airplane was too small for the number of people coming aboard. I could feel myself starting to panic a little.

I was trying to stay calm, but when the flight attendant started to pull the hatch door closed, it seemed as if the plane walls started closing in and I couldn't get enough air to breathe. In that moment, I lost it and yelled, "No! Don't close the door!" Of course, she came right over to me to see what my problem was. I was able to convince her that I was just hot and wanted a little bit more of the air conditioning before the door was closed. She was kind and understanding, but she also kept one eye on me throughout the flight. The fact that I was fine one minute and felt like I was going to die the next instantly ruined flying for me.

I was so scared about flying over the ocean. I brought my headphones and some music to help zone me out. I put them on and started hearing Coldplay, which both Bryce and I loved. I instantly felt like I was going to die. I thought I was going to have a heart attack. I had actual physical chest pain. I pulled the headphones off and was afraid to listen to any music after that.

I thought that I would die on the flight and imagined crashing into the ocean. All sorts of bad thoughts were racing through my head. Then I started talking to God. "Please help Bryce. Please help Bryce." But then in my fear and frustration I just said, "Forget it. Do what you're going to do. Kill me too. I'm good."

Suddenly all the fear started leaving me. Once I got to the point where I was totally ready to die, I wasn't afraid anymore. I still stayed awake the entire flight, but the fear was gone.

I landed at the Tokyo Haneda Airport for a middle-of-the-night layover. Once inside the airport, my phone rang; it was Dr. Julian Wright, the 35th Medical Group Chief of Medical Staff, overseeing Bryce's care. Part of his role was to help facilitate the communication between the Japanese hospital staff taking care of Bryce, the Misawa Air Force Base Wing Commander, and me. This was the first time I had the chance to talk to a doctor about Bryce's condition.

"Hey, Mrs. Powers," he said in a caring tone. "How was your flight? There's been no change."

"What happened to him?" I asked.

"I don't really know all the details. He has a severe head injury. He's got some lung injuries, and he's being taken care of in the regional Japanese trauma center ICU. He's in critical condition and can't be moved. I know it will help when you get here."

Still feeling a bit confused about who was actually driving when the accident happened, I asked him if he knew if Bryce was the driver or the passenger. He said Bryce was the driver. So I only had that relief that Bryce wasn't driving (and possibly in trouble) from LAX to Tokyo. Maybe God let this miscommunication happen to get me through the flight across the ocean.

As I looked around, at first I saw only Asian people. Then moments later, I saw a Caucasian man and woman who looked worried sick. I started freaking out, wondering if they were the other injured AMMO airman's parents. Then I saw them getting into the airplane with me. We never talked to each other, but I watched them closely. I don't think they ever even knew I was there or who I was.

An hour later, we landed in Misawa. The military personnel were waiting for us, holding up one sign with my name and another sign with the name, "Wade." I saw the man look at the sign and nod, and I knew they were the other parents. I was worried they were going to be angry or start yelling at me. They looked like how I felt.

I watched the other couple pick up their luggage, and I couldn't stop thinking, "Oh my gosh! We are going to be in the same car in just a minute. What's going to happen? Are they going to start crying? Did their child die?"

I had been awake from the time I left Charlotte on Saturday, October 13, and now it was Monday, October 15. It seemed like Bryce's accident was years ago. Everything was confusing.

Once we passed through security, I met Lieutenant Colonel Branch and First Sergeant Jackson, and received my first two hugs in Japan.

I was then introduced to my Family Liaison Officer (FLO), Kendra Odell, who was appointed to assist me in this new land, and Robert Hanson, who was assigned to help the Wades. It was explained that if we needed anything, had any questions, or any concerns whatsoever, they were there to provide assistance and support to us. I learned later that they had both been handpicked for this mission. Kendra's regular job in the military was a "crack checker," which basically meant she inspected airplanes, looking closely for any cracks in the body or wings. After the brief introductions, together we climbed into a van, and they drove us to the trauma hospital first, so we could see our kids.

First Sergeant Jackson helped me fill out the Japanese forms required to receive an ICU visitor pass, and then took me in to see Bryce.

The first thing I did was to reach for his hand and give him a three-squeeze "coma hug." It was amazing. It was not planned, it was just spontaneous. I was wondering, "Does he know that it's me? Does he get it? Does he remember our 'coma hug'?" I just acted normal. I tried not to freak out or cry in front of him. "Hi, Bryce, it's Mom. I'm here. Everything's okay."

Facebook Update: Monday 10/15/12

Thank you to everyone that has been praying for our son, Bryce! He needs our prayers more than ever! I was able to see him today, hold his hand and tell him how much I love him.

I told him how much we all love him and that many people are praying for him to get better. It was extremely difficult to see him lying there, motionless, as he remains in a coma and on a ventilator.

Biggest concerns right now: He has several fractures in his head, bleeding in his brain, and lung contusions.

The Air Force has been so kind to me. They flew me out here within hours of the accident. They picked me up from the airport. They assigned an Air Force representative to help me get set up with lodging. They filled the room and refrigerator with food and drinks, and they are providing daily hot meals prepared by the squadron and AMMO troop families. They are also driving me back and forth to the hospital, which is about an hour drive each way. They are doing everything in their power to help me through this very difficult time. You can clearly see how much they care about Bryce!

Today the Air Force gave me a computer to borrow so I won't have to try and use my phone to share our updates. The Air Force personnel have been a great help! So please, just keep passing the word for others to pray. Thank you.

I don't mind receiving messages at all. I appreciate the love and prayers... and when I can't sleep, I log-in and read your beautiful and supportive words. Love you all! Cathy

Life Offline

In my imagination, I thought Bryce would be all mangled up, like something I had seen on TV. But when I walked in to his room, it looked like he was just sleeping. He just looked beautiful. There were no gashes. He was on the respirator, and he looked a little swollen. He did have what is known as "battle sign bruising" behind his ears, and there was blood coming out of his ears.

His fingernails were full of mud and blood, which seemed weird to me. Bryce was not the kind of person to have dirty hands and nails. I did get an opportunity to wash it off of him, but it still freaked me out. I was also upset that he had blood left on him. It really bothered me. Why did they leave him like this?

He didn't move for the first few days. Then he began the "caveman" automatic-type posturing, which I later learned was a sign of a severe brain injury. I never did get used to this.

Facebook Update: Tuesday 10/16/12

So thankful I was able to spend a lot of time with Bryce today. The nurses were just wonderful and they allowed me to stay with him for eight straight hours. In Japan the hospitals are run very differently than in the U.S. At this particular hospital, you get two hours to visit in the morning, and four hours to visit in the afternoon. That's it.

Today, the nurse asked me, with the help of a Japanese/English translation book, if I would like to work with her to wash Bryce's hair, brush his teeth, shave him, and clean him up. Of course I said, "Yes." She wrapped my arm in plastic, which is in a cast because I broke my wrist a couple weeks ago, and then we washed him together. It was special to be able to do something to help him.

Today I met with Dr. Toshiyuki Karumai, one of the Japanese doctors treating Bryce. He shared, with the help of a translator, the extent of damage to his body more clearly. He told me that Bryce seriously damaged his brainstem and that his early prognosis is that Bryce "will be a vegetable."

He also talked about the seriousness of his lung contusions and the bleeding in his lungs, explaining it will take quite a while for them to heal. Bryce is also leaking cerebrospinal fluid from his nose and ears. He explained it is due to the fractures in his skull, and hopefully it will stop as the bones fuse back together.

Okay, that was a lot of bad news. I will now share some of the good news of the day.

Two of Bryce's AMMO friends came out to the hospital to visit him today. Their Lieutenant Colonel brought them in. They talked to him a little bit and stood by his side. I could clearly see how much they were torn up about all that happened. It was a very sweet meeting.

After they left, I got a tissue to wipe away some of the fluid that was dripping from Bryce's nose. At the exact moment that I touched his nose, Bryce's main ICU nurse, Yuko Yamamoto, and I saw Bryce's eye twitch ever so little. An hour later when we were washing his hair, Yuko and I saw Bryce's mouth and lips slightly move. A few minutes later, when she began pulling some of the tape around the ventilator off his face, he slightly lifted up his left hand, made a fist, and then continued to lift his hand a tiny bit higher. A few seconds later he lifted his right hand too, and seemed like maybe he was trying to grab for his face to make us stop. Yuko was smiling, and saying, "Very good, very good, very good", in English! I was beside myself with happiness, and Dr. Karumai agreed that this could indeed be very good news.

They are planning to do an MRI on Bryce, and that will show them a much clearer picture of his brain and the damage. However, at this point, we must patiently wait until he is stable enough to be moved. Dr. Karumai said it could be a couple more weeks before he can be safely moved and left in an MRI machine for the forty-plus minutes they need to run the test.

I'm doing my best to not let my mind wander, making a deliberate choice to keep trusting God to heal him. Please continue to pray and believe with me.

Love you all so much, Cathy.

Life Offline

Sarah Wade was fresh out of tech school and had just recently arrived in Misawa. This was her first duty station. She had been assigned to work in the AMMO dump front office, which is where she and Bryce met. They had only been friends for a short amount of time when this tragic accident happened.

I got to know her parents a little bit as we talked during the one-hour drive from the hospital to the base. They had worked as educators in another country for many years and said their daughter had lived outside the United States for more years of her life than inside. They were a lovely couple, and I was so happy when I learned they were also Christians.

In the middle of one conversation with Sarah's mother I just blurted out, "I'm so sorry. I don't even know what happened. My son is a good kid. When I found out Bryce was driving, I felt ashamed and scared."

The dad looked at the mom and kind of nodded. "We originally heard Sarah was driving," she said. "We know that feeling because we experienced the same thing. We just found out back in Tokyo that someone else was driving."

So I started crying, and Sarah's mom wiped away a tear or two. We didn't know all the facts surrounding the accident.

Chapter Two

Hopeful Signs

And so I began my months-long quest for hopeful signs regarding Bryce's condition. Every flicker of his eyelid, every response to a request from me or one of the nurses brought a small shaft of light into a heart that was devastated by my son's bleak prognosis. Despite the horror of it all, the day-to-day details of Bryce's life needed my attention, and so I pressed on through the haze, not knowing what challenges each day would bring.

I closed Bryce's Skype and Xbox Live accounts. I was also able to turn off his cable, Internet, personal cell phone, and a few other miscellaneous online gaming subscriptions. I didn't want them to keep charging him the monthly fees, but I had such a huge lump in my throat. Ugh.

I spoke with Jim to give him an update on Bryce's condition. He told me that everything was going well at home and that my friend Gwyn would be arriving in Japan within twenty-four hours. Gwyn and I have been best friends for many years, so Jim arranged with the Air Force to have her travel to Japan to be a support to me. I was looking forward to having my friend by my side through those dark days.

After visiting Bryce at the hospital, my driver took me to the base so I could get some things from Bryce's dorm room. Being surrounded by his things was extremely comforting to me. I saw his coffee cup next to his Keurig machine, with a little bit of pumpkin spice coffee still in his cup. I guess it was his last cup of coffee from the morning of October 13. I had sent him a care package full of K-Cups, cookies, and other treats a month before. I was glad to see he had been enjoying them. Above his computer, Bryce had displayed our last family portrait in a black frame, which was nice to see.

I lay down in his bed and pulled the covers over my head for a while. It smelled exactly like him. My world was spinning. Bryce was living his dream in this room just a couple of days ago. Now I had no idea what his future held. Suddenly I was overcome with sadness and emotional pain. I wished I could snap my fingers and turn back the clock.

At the time, I was much more worried that Bryce was going to be in trouble for the accident than that he was not getting better. Maybe I did this to protect myself from the reality of his injuries. I prayed for God's mercy, protection, and favor in Bryce's situation.

I thought for sure he would wake up and be okay. I also prayed for a healing miracle for Sarah. I hated that Bryce was the driver and now she was in a coma and on a ventilator.

I found myself trying to work a deal with God. It would only be fair for God to heal Sarah first, since she was the passenger and it wasn't her fault. Then I hoped, of course, that God would heal and restore Bryce, too. Trying to work everything out in my own mind gave me a horrible headache and my heart hurt with a crushing sensation. I was feeling overwhelmed and I had to force myself to stay calm. After a short while, I got up and busied myself looking around the room again.

I came upon a stack of Bryce's mail on a shelf above his coffeepot. He had letters and cards from us and a few of his friends that he had saved in a nice little pile. I carefully opened the cards and letters that were from me. It was heart-wrenching and yet strangely satisfying to reread what I had sent him. I was so glad I told him, "I love you!" over and over again when I wrote.

I was also happy that I regularly told him Jesus loved him. I told him to keep trusting God for his future and that I was always praying for him. Reading these brought me some peace—and I needed peace desperately.

I didn't know if Bryce had been to church in Japan. I know he went to church services in boot camp, because that was one of the only ways to get out of the difficult training. I also knew this because Bryce told me it was great. He loved to sing and worship in the services, and he said it was a powerful experience. I was worried about him as he laid suspended between life and death in a coma, and wondered if he was still doing okay spiritually.

Suddenly I noticed a brand-new Bible lying open in front of his computer keyboard. I picked it up, admiring the cool two-tone cover. I had so many thoughts racing through my mind.

Where did he get this? How long has he been studying God's Word again?

I eventually closed it, and to this day I wish I could remember what page it had been opened to. But this experience of seeing his new Bible lying open brought me a sense of hope and peace. I cleaned his room and even took out a big bag of pizza boxes, beverage bottles, and trash. He had a collection of empty beer bottles that were all perfectly lined up across his desk and shelves. The drinking age in Japan is twenty, so he was of legal age, but I was still a little uneasy when I saw them. He had been in Japan ten months so far, so the twenty to twenty-five bottles could have all been his, but I just hoped Bryce was having an occasional beer with a meal and nothing more serious.

I made his bed and sorted his dirty laundry. Then I got on his computer to pay a couple of his bills using his money. I sent some emails and then shut down his computer.

When all the work was done, I sat in his office chair just staring at his things for what seemed like a long time. The reality and seriousness of what was happening to Bryce literally took my breath away. I grabbed Benjamin, Bryce's little white gorilla that was sitting on his desk shelf. I knew he was a tough military man, but I thought maybe Bryce would like to have his favorite stuffed animal friend close to him. I also took some of Bryce's special sentimental possessions, including his high school class ring, his camera, and his military challenge coins.

Later, my FLO brought me to my hotel, which was within walking distance of Bryce's dorm room. There was a beautiful bouquet of flowers on the table with a note addressed to me from Bryce's Commander. I remember thinking that these people really cared. I was thankful to be there and was hoping and praying Bryce would be okay.

Facebook Update: Thursday 10/18/12, 5:00 a.m.

My wonderful friend, Gwyn, made it to Misawa safely yesterday. She was flown here by the Air Force to be a support person for me since Jim and Madison had to stay behind. Gwyn has known and loved Bryce since he was a young boy. Our families have been amazingly close. We have supported each other for many years. Gwyn's husband, Tom, is a retired Master Chief in the U.S. Coast Guard, and one of her four children is also in the Air Force, serving in Germany.

We spent the day with Bryce, sitting by his bedside, holding his hands and telling him how much we love him. We also told him that so many of his friends, family, and even strangers, new friends from a prayer page on Facebook, are praying for him around the clock.

It was interesting that when I spoke to him, his blood pressure and heart rate would start to rise. Yuko, with a big smile on her face pointed to her ears and said, "Very good. He hear you, Momma!" Then she pointed to the numbers and through a translator said, "They go up when Momma talk." This made me feel so happy! Poor kid, it was nonstop chattering after I had that info (lol).

Dr. Karumai tried to lower his sedation level yesterday to see how Bryce would react. He began posturing, which is a sign of brain injury. So they had to turn his sedation level back up to give his brain more time to heal.

Gwyn and I, along with the doctors and nurses, witnessed Bryce moving his head, neck, hands and arms in what appeared to be an intentional manner. It almost always happened when they were doing something that bothered him, or caused him pain, though a couple of times he just randomly moved.

One good sign is that even though Bryce still needs a ventilator, he has now begun to breathe on his own. If I understand correctly, the ventilator gives him a push, introducing air under pressure to help him breathe in, but the breathing impulses are all coming from him. His oxygen saturation is one hundred percent.

No one can predict medically what will happen with Bryce's healing, and how far he will eventually recover. So since they don't know, I'm going with God and the whole miracle route. I believe he will be healed completely!

Over the past few years, I have repeatedly heard the term, "hurry up and wait" in connection with the military. It's ironic that his prognosis seems to fall right in with that unofficial motto.

Thank you all so much for your continued prayers for Bryce! They are working! Please don't stop! I love and appreciate each of you! Gwyn says, "Hi!"

Love, Cathy

Life Offline

Over the next few days, things started becoming more complicated between me and Sarah's parents. On our third day in Japan, we met in the lobby of the hotel and Jackson told us we would be meeting with the Judge Advocate General (JAG), which is the military lawyer. They set up a private meeting area in our hotel. I asked Gwyn to join me in the conference room with the JAG, while the Wades waited for their turn in the lobby.

When we got to see the lawyer, he let me know that there were no drugs or alcohol involved, and that Bryce had his seat belt on. But he also said that there was possible reckless driving involved, and they were trying to get to the bottom of exactly what happened.

Instantly I began feeling nauseous. It was already horrible seeing Bryce at the brink of death, and now he might be in trouble when he wakes up. No one was pointing a finger, but just the thought of more bad news for Bryce was more than I thought I could handle.

Two valuable airmen, who were technically government property, had been seriously injured in a car accident, so I completely understood the need for a full military investigation.

I was also told it was a beautiful sunny day, so the road conditions were fine. There were no citations issued by the Japanese or military police. So now we had to wait for the investigation to be completed before getting any more answers.

I was worried sick about all of the possibilities, and yet they told me not to worry until I had something to worry about. So we discussed some of the worst-case scenarios. There was a long list of "what-if's," including a number of possible short-term and long-term consequences. Everything depended on what happened.

I quietly begged God for His mercy on Bryce's life.

"Bryce could be sued if certain things happened," the lawyer explained, "depending on injuries, death, or damages. Bryce is twenty years old and has a good record. He wasn't doing anything that another twenty-year-old wouldn't do, and the military won't be able to say that he did anything on purpose to hurt anyone.

"You have to ask yourself, did Bryce get into his car thinking that he would go out and hurt himself or others? The answer to that is no. And it would be hard to prove otherwise. But we are in another country, and we have to respect their rules. So, unfortunately, this is going to take some time to sort out."

I asked him what would happen next and how long we would have to wait to get the "in the line of duty" designation.

"I don't know exactly," he answered. "Every case is different. But Bryce has the right to an attorney."

I learned a little bit about what the "in the line of duty" designation is. The simple explanation: If a service member purposefully chooses to partake in a high risk, or questionable behavior, and in doing so suffers injuries, illness, or death, they will most likely not receive an "in the line of duty" designation.

This is a very serious consequence because any residual injuries, or long term disabilities, would not be covered medically. The military does pay for the initial injuries sustained, but once the service member is discharged, the veteran becomes responsible for ongoing medical bills. These high risk activities can include a wide array of extreme sports, recklessness, and both illegal and legal behaviors.

Now, if it was his day off and he went to the beach stepped on a broken bottle, and cut off his toe, the incident would be considered "in the line of duty." This injury, and its repercussions, would be covered medically for the rest of his life because it was merely an accident.

The Department of Veterans Affairs system and the active duty military medical structure state that serious accidents, injuries, and illnesses, must be investigated, and determined "in the line of duty," or future care may not be covered. So, if Bryce did not receive that designation, he would not receive any type of future medical coverage, and that was scary.

At that point, we didn't know if he had done anything wrong. That's why the drug and alcohol tests coming back negative and the fact that his seat belt was on were so important.

Was he speeding? Was he being reckless? We didn't know yet, and the answers to these questions could impact the rest of our lives.

The JAG promised to try to find some answers. "I'll try to find an attorney who can help you when you get back to the states. Let me see if I can also find someone near your hometown in North Carolina, so we can all tag team to get you the help and answers you need."

He also went over Bryce's living will, power of attorney, and all the other legal forms. Fortunately, from his own experience in the military, Jim knew he had to have a serious conversation with Bryce before he left for boot camp. He told Bryce to make sure he put his Momma's name on everything. I took Bryce to a lawyer before he left to go overseas, and we had all of his paperwork in order. Bryce also gave me all of his passwords in case of an emergency.

I was afraid there could be legal consequences. We drove back to the base with Sarah's parents that evening. Then the next day everything started getting weird. Neither of her parents were making eye contact with me, and we were separated into two fifteen-passenger vans from that point forward.

I started overthinking everything and freaking out. I should have been concerned about the fact that Bryce was not waking up and could possibly die, but it was always these smaller things that bothered me. I felt like everything was spinning out of control. I thought they were going to sue Bryce or our family. I thought Bryce was going to jail.

The lawyer stated that the AMMO troop driving in front of Bryce said they were "testing the handling of their cars." The military police initially said the driver "incriminated himself" because the airman wrote out the word "drifting" in his written statement. Since drifting is illegal, it was used against him as soon as he passed it to the military police.

If Sarah died from her injuries and Bryce was found to be at fault, he could be charged. All of this news was just horrible and just more stuff to worry about. I was told one story by the person driving in front of Bryce, and the police were told another story. Unfortunately, without Bryce and Sarah having the ability to tell us what happened, we just didn't know.

After 2 days of pure hell in the hospital with no more contact with the Wades, Gwyn, without my permission or knowledge, approached Sarah's dad. "I know you guys are Christians. Are you planning to sue Cathy and her family?"

Sarah's dad said, "What do you mean?"

Gwyn told him I was not eating, not sleeping, and crying all the time because I was so upset. "Cathy is already so worried about Bryce being in a coma. She doesn't even know I'm asking you, but are you going to sue her? Please just tell me your plans so at least she'll know if she's worrying about something that she doesn't have to."

Sarah's dad looked in her eyes and said, "I can't imagine a situation where that would happen."

Gwyn came back to the ICU to tell me what Mr. Wade said. Only a few minutes later. Sarah's dad walked in and approached Bryce's bed. I looked up, and he had tears in his eyes. He said, "I am so sorry. I am so sorry."

I was thinking, "Oh my God, Sarah's dead."

"We didn't know," he said through his tears. "We didn't know." And then he started crying, and wiping his face with a tissue.

I was so confused. "What didn't you know?"

"We didn't know; we just found out."

"Found out what?"

"About the helicopter."

"What helicopter?"

"The Japanese helicopter landed, and they could have taken both of them, but they only took Sarah, and they left Bryce. I'm so sorry he didn't get that medical care."

I started to freak out on the inside, but I remained quiet. Without saying anything else, Sarah's dad left the room. I'm sure I looked dazed and confused.

Soon after, Dr. Wright came in to check on Bryce. I was no longer able to keep quiet about the news of the helicopter, and I asked him if it was true. As soon as I asked about the helicopter, he just stiffened right up.

"Yes, ma'am., uhh, but I'm not really sure why that happened."

I wasn't really getting much information from the military, and it was frustrating. I learned little things on my own, from the airmen on base or from the Japanese hospital staff, and then tried to find more detailed information from the military liaisons. I don't think it was on purpose, but communication and trying to piece together specific details was difficult at times. I was only getting bits and pieces of information when I desperately wanted to know all the specifics. It took a while to sort it all out.

Eventually, I learned that a Japanese medical helicopter had landed at the accident scene to transport the patients to the nearest trauma center, an hour away in Hachinohe, Japan. I was told they had room for both.

They loaded Sarah in to the helicopter first. But when they went to get Bryce, one of the American medics said, "He's probably drunk and passed out. Just take him back to the base. He'll most likely be fine."

It was then decided Bryce would not be transported by helicopter to the trauma hospital, but instead he was taken to the small base clinic in a Japanese ambulance.

He had gone into respiratory arrest in that ambulance. The medics did not have the supplies or training to intubate him and could not give Bryce the oxygen he desperately needed. Then at the base hospital it had taken three intubation attempts to get the oxygen flowing to his body again. No one knows exactly how long he went without receiving the optimum levels of oxygen to his brain.

There is a "golden hour" in the care of trauma patients. Sadly, during those vital sixty minutes, Bryce did not get what he needed, and he arrived at the hospital on the edge of death.

Then something amazing happened.

Chapter Three

The First Miracle

Facebook Update: Friday 10/19/12

Sarah woke up today after several days in an induced coma. What an absolute miracle!

Life Offline

In the beginning I thought Sarah's injuries were the same as Bryce's, except that she also had a spleen injury. So I called Jim to tell him the exciting news that she had woken up.

The Dr. Karumai came by with Dr. Wright, and they both told me what a miracle it was. I remember feeling a wave of relief. This news seemed to be a game changer. I was so happy and relieved, thinking that any time now it would be Bryce's turn.

I had worried that maybe it was Bryce's fault she was in a coma, and I was so glad she was going to be okay. I was genuinely happy for her and thankful to God for healing her the way he did. Yet at the same time, Bryce's condition remained the same. I shared this update on Bryce's Facebook prayer page the same day that Sarah woke up:

Facebook Update: Friday 10/19/12

Today was a quiet day for Bryce. His pupils are still non-reactive, and two different sizes, one large, and one small. Periodically, his heart rate drops too low, sounding the alarm, and they have to raise his sedation level to get it back into a more normal range.

He is still having swelling in his brain, and also leakage of cerebrospinal fluid from his nose and ears. It is so hard to see this happening. He desperately needs our prayers!

On a brighter note, we saw two signs that seemed to be encouraging. With that said, everyone has a different opinion and interpretation of what might be happening.

First, the nurses were attempting to change the tape and mouthpiece for Bryce's ventilator. When doing this, they were having trouble getting his mouth opened far enough to insert a new bite guard. Anyway, they were struggling like crazy, and I told Bryce to open his mouth, and instantly his mouth opened ever so slightly for them to insert it.

We were all amazed, but not sure if it was intentional or a reflex. Unfortunately the mouth guard was not in the correct position, and they needed to shift the placement just a little. Once again I asked him to open his mouth for the nurses, and it opened slightly for a second time. What are the odds that this would happen two times?

Second, several times a day Bryce's eyelashes are gently touched to see if there is any reaction. Today, closely following his mouth incident, when they were touched, his eye flinched slightly. The nurses were very excited and told us this was a good sign. I hope this is true, and these are indeed good signs. Lord God, please heal Bryce!

Love, Cathy

Life Offline

I seriously was thinking that at any moment Bryce would just open his eyes, see me, and say something like, "What are you doing here in Japan, Momma?" Isn't that the way it always happens on TV and in the movies? So why not for us? I was praying so hard for a quick miracle recovery to unfold before us.

Facebook Update: Saturday 10/20/12

Bryce had to have his ventilator turned back on to full power. Last night he was struggling to breathe and his heart rate kept dropping, so the doctors had to help him out. He had been breathing on his own impulse, with just a little help from the ventilator for the last few days, but he now needs a rest.

He is also having an adverse reaction to one or more of his medications and has a blistering rash on his body. His tongue and lips are swollen too. He had a rash earlier this week, so they switched a few of his medications, but the results now are worse. Hopefully changing his medications again will solve this.

Bryce's sedation levels had to be raised a few levels today as well. He was posturing, over and over. His medical team is hoping a deeper sedation will ease the amount of times this posturing happens. That is my prayer.

Love, Cathy

Life Offline

Today I paid off Bryce's VISA credit card using money from his bank account. Thank goodness he added me onto his bank before leaving home. I know if I felt like my hands were tied it would make this all so much worse. I'm glad I'm able to help him. I'm thankful we had a contingency plan to take care of his obligations if anything were to ever happen to him. Even so, it's still hard. I keep reminding myself of how happy he'll be when he wakes up and finds he still has great credit!

Facebook Update: Sunday 10/21/12

I wanted to take a moment and share how thankful I am for the incredible team of Japanese and American medical staff taking care of Bryce. Seriously, the care Bryce is receiving in Japan is amazing. The nurses are so kind, loving, and meticulous in their care. They seem to go out of their way to do everything in their power to keep him comfortable, clean, and infection free.

The doctors are all Japanese, except for one incredible Air Force doctor, Dr. Wright, a pathologist, who speaks Japanese. He is our Air Force medical liaison. I'm pretty sure he stays in daily contact with the Japanese doctors. I have never in my life seen this level of caring in a hospital situation. Sometimes the language barriers make it difficult to communicate, but we all have special dictionaries to get our concerns across.

Gwyn and I visited Calvary Baptist this morning here in Misawa, a church Bryce recently visited. It was a blessing to be surrounded by such loving people. The members were so friendly and the pastor said a very special prayer of healing. Also, the church members have been busy making one-thousand origami cranes for Bryce, and one-thousand more for Sarah. These cranes, if I understand correctly, are a Japanese custom. They are used both in times of tragedy, and in times of celebration. The folded cranes are each personalized. Some have prayers or Bible verses, while others contain "get-well" wishes. When the one-thousand cranes have been completed, they will be strung together, and displayed.

Life Offline

The pastor of Calvary Baptist Church, Bruce Truss, and his compassionate wife came to the ICU in Hachinohe to see us and pray for Bryce. Until a few days ago, when an Air Force chaplain praying for Bryce had mentioned it to me, I had no idea Bryce had visited their church and recently attended a Bible study. Knowing that Bryce is still chasing after the Lord brings me great comfort.

Facebook Update: Monday 10/22/12

Today was a somber day. I don't understand what is happening with Bryce. His allergic rash has returned and is now all over his body. His lips and tongue have swollen again, and his blood pressure and heart rate were high all day. The cerebrospinal fluid was leaking all day too. His sedation medication was doubled yesterday, and today was tripled.

I'm not a doctor, I'm his Momma, but all of these signs together make my heart heavy. He needs a miracle. Please continue to lift him up in prayer.

Tomorrow Bryce is having a surgery to move his breathing tube from his mouth to his neck. The procedure is called a tracheostomy. This will allow him to breathe a bit easier. Right now on the ventilator, it is like breathing through a straw. The body gets tired having to do this much work.

Every family has little endearments or customs that are unique to them. In our family, ever since Bryce and Madison were little, we had two major family rules.

The first was a secret numeric code, only known by us, and it was drilled into them that no one could pick them up in an emergency situation without it! Unless the person knew our secret code, the kids knew not to go with them, or trust them. We actually used this in a couple of situations over the years.

The second was what we called the COMA HUG. The COMA HUG came about because I wanted to have a plan that would enable us to communicate our love for each other without words. The way we planned it, I would hold their hand in mine, and squeeze it three times, which meant, "I love you!" Each squeeze represents one word. The kids would then squeeze my hand back four times, which meant, "I love you, too!" We have practiced this for years, in movie theaters, church services, even at bedtimes. When Bryce was last home on leave, I gave him numerous COMA HUGs, and each time, he responded in kind.

While having a child in a coma is a parent's absolute worst nightmare, it brought me a little peace knowing that we have a contingency plan for just this. Last Monday when I arrived at Bryce's bedside, I immediately gave him a three squeeze COMA HUG, and I have repeated it numerous times every day since. I continually pray that someday soon I will feel his hand squeeze back. I hope this story blesses you.

Love, Cathy

Life Offline

My head just spins when I think about our coma hug contingency plan. We have been practicing the drill for two decades, just in case one of us was to ever be in a real coma. I sure hope Bryce can feel my three squeezes. "I" squeeze, "love" squeeze, "you" squeeze!

Facebook Update: Tuesday 10/23/12

Bryce's tracheostomy went very well today. I am so happy he had it because he seems to be breathing more easily.

We found out this afternoon that the rash on his body is not an allergic reaction. The dermatologist came by to examine it and said that because Bryce's immune system is low right now, he has a skin staph infection, which is being treated. They didn't seem to be alarmed by it, so I won't worry either.

Love, Cathy

Facebook Update: Wednesday 10/24/12

I am absolutely encouraged! Today when we got to the ICU to see Bryce, we were just amazed out how good he looked. His color was good. His blood pressure and heart rate was back in the target range. He had no fever. His staph infection was a light pink and clearing up. His lips were almost back to normal. For the first time since his accident on October 13, we saw what looks like an improvement.

Yesterday, I asked that everyone pray for the cerebrospinal fluid to stop leaking, and also for the pressure to go down. It looks like our prayers have been answered. Bryce did not leak any cerebrospinal fluid all day long! I am so grateful for this answer to prayer.

Love, Cathy

Life Offline

Here is something interesting about Japanese hospitals: you are expected to bring your own supplies. They gave me a list, in Japanese, of things I needed to purchase and bring to the ICU for Bryce. They requested Bryce's razor, toothpaste, toothbrush, shampoo, soap, lotion, pads, diapers, some medications that could be purchased downstairs in the hospital store, and a long list of all sorts of other things. This was definitely a different experience than a typical American hospital stay. I was blessed because the Air Force and AMMO flight took the list and made sure Bryce had everything he needed that I was not able to bring from his dorm room on base.

Facebook Update: Friday 10/26/12

This morning, Dr. Karumai and a neurosurgeon inserted a lumbar shunt into Bryce's lower spine to help relieve some of his cranial pressure. The plan for the next several days is to simply let Bryce rest and heal.

Thank you for your love and prayers!

Love, Cathy

Facebook Update: Saturday 10/27/12

Gwyn and I stand on each side of Bryce's bed and we hold his hands, talk to him gently, and pray over him. Gwyn has been reading to him from her Kindle. Today we finished our first book, "Heaven Is For Real," written by Lynn Vincent and Todd Burpo. The book was extremely inspirational and uplifting for us because it is about a little boy near death who had the experience of going to Heaven, seeing Jesus, and meeting some of his relatives. It's a beautiful story.

I hope Bryce was able to hear and comprehend the story, and that it brought him comfort. I pray Bryce is having his own special time with Jesus right now, without pain, fear, or any worries.

On a personal note, I am very sad today. This is so hard. I miss my son. The Bryce I know is a funny, animated, loving, goofy, twenty-year-old young man. Of course I know this is still Bryce. It's just so heartbreaking to not see any sign of his personality.

I know I can't fix this myself, and I can't control how this is all going to turn out either. All I can do is place my trust in a loving God, keep praying, and keep walking forward. I'm trying my best to be transparent and real with you, but I want you to know that I am not ever giving up on my son and his recovery! I thank you for praying for him to be fully restored!

It is a good thing we are going to church tomorrow. Gwyn and I need a fresh dose of God's Word, and His love. Always praying for that big miracle too!

Love, Cathy

Facebook Update: Sunday 10/28/12

Bryce is back on the ventilator again. His body was holding on to too much carbon dioxide, and he wasn't taking enough breaths per minute, so they are giving him the extra breaths he needs. Hopefully this will help his body rest.

Today, I believe God gave me a special gift, and I saw a glimpse of the old Bryce. Before the accident, Bryce has always had a cute "pouty face" in which he roles his lips a certain way when he was in trouble or in pain or sad. This afternoon, I looked at him and saw that famous "pouty face." Of course, no mother wants to see their child sad or in pain, but believe me, seeing this old familiar trait sure brought my heart joy. It gave me new hope that I will see more of my Bryce in the future.

Thank you so much for all your love and prayers! They are certainly working!

Love, Cathy

Life Offline

Madison sent me this message:

"I read your post today and it scared me really bad. What's going on? I thought he was doing better."

I knew I had to reassure her everything was okay. I wrote back:

"Don't worry Madi, God is with him, and so am I. I will take care of him. I love and miss you my sweet and precious Madi Belle, Love you, Hugs, Momma."

Sarah is healing at a much faster pace than Bryce. I'm thankful and relieved she is getting stronger every day, and I will continue to pray for her body, mind, and spirit until she is fully healed. I look at Bryce and wonder if he is going to be up and walking in a few more days too. They were in the same car, after all. I hope he wakes up soon

.

Chapter Four

Why Won't He Wake Up?

Facebook Update: Monday 10/29/12

The most important thing for Bryce right now is for his fractures to heal, and for the cerebrospinal fluid to stop leaking. The reason this is so important is because there is an increased risk of infection to his brain through the leakage and cracks. Even a small infection entering through his nose or ears could be very dangerous.

Dr. Karumai was able to insert a new feeding tube that bypasses his stomach, and goes all the way down to his intestine. His original feeding tube will now be used as a vent to help relieve any pressure that builds up in his stomach, which will make him more comfortable. For over two weeks now, Bryce has been unable to hold down his milkshake meals, so I am very glad they were able to do this for him today.

Love, Cathy

Facebook Update: Tuesday 10/30/12

While today is his seventeenth day in a coma, there is still plenty of room for hope. Bryce is surrounded by a great staff of doctors, both Japanese and American, and nurses who take fantastic care of him.

This hospital is very different than any hospitals I have visited in the U.S. It's interesting to see the differences in customs.

One interesting fact about the Japanese ICU is that we cannot simply walk into Bryce's room without following a strict protocol. We are first required to remove our shoes and place them into lockers. We are then provided with a pair of sterile slippers. Lastly, we decontaminate our hands with a disinfectant that is dispensed when we step on a foot pedal. Only after we follow this protocol are we permitted to enter the hospital's clean zone.

We are expected to leave the ICU every day from 1:00 to 3:00 pm. During this time, we go to the family room. Inside this room, we don't wear the sterile slippers. Socks are the appropriate foot attire here. The hospital provides personal mats for us to sit on, and low, rectangular tables for us to set our food on while we eat. In addition to eating, most in the family room are watching the television. Of course, Gwyn and I have no idea what they are saying. Even so, it's entertaining as we try to guess what's happening.

After eating, many people lie on their mats and take a nap until the visiting hours resume. I remember the first couple of days here, thinking this behavior was so strange. I was uncomfortable seeing strangers sound asleep on the floor around me. After a few days, I tried it myself, and not only did those awkward feelings go away, I now look forward to this extra time of rest.

Sarah came to the ICU with her mother to visit Bryce. It sure was nice to see her wide awake with a beautiful smile on her face! She will be leaving Japan tomorrow, heading back to the United States for rehabilitation. Her recovery thus far has been nothing short of a miracle! She spent almost six days lying silent in a coma, and now she is wide awake and talking! It's exciting to think about Bryce waking up soon too. I can hardly stand the wait!

Her mom stepped back and stayed a few feet from the foot of Bryce's bed. I was standing up by Bryce's head, also on his right side. I said hi to Sarah and asked her how she was doing. She smiled and seemed very shy, and maybe answered with a word or two, saying she was good. I told her how happy I was that she was awake and doing so well and that I had been praying for her. I told her I believed it was a miracle. She just sat in that chair beaming with a beautiful, bright smile.

I looked up at her mom and noticed she was silently bawling. Tears were just streaming down her face; she tried to, but couldn't even speak. I couldn't tell if she was happy crying or sad crying. I was so uncomfortable, not knowing if she was upset that Sarah was injured or upset that Bryce hadn't woken up. I started to walk toward her, wanting to comfort her, and then she put up her arm and motioned that she'd be back, and she left the ICU.

Sarah was still smiling, shyly looking between me and Bryce and around the room and then back at Bryce, staring from his head to his feet. I had no idea what she was thinking or what she understood. I felt so bad for all she had been through. I was afraid to bring up the accident. Instead, I told her I had heard she was a great influence on Bryce and thanked her for talking to Bryce about God, helping him to get back on track with going to church, and buying a new Bible. She continued to look around and smile, and then her mom walked in and wheeled her away.

I wondered what she understood at that point. Her mom and dad told me that Sarah didn't know she'd been in an accident yet. She had recently had her tonsils removed, so when she woke up from her coma, she thought she was waking up from that surgery. She couldn't believe her parents came to Japan for her tonsillectomy. Even though she had tubes coming out of her and a neck brace, she did not have any idea that she had been in a car accident or that anything else was wrong with her.

This was very strange to me then, but now I have a better understanding of the TBI world. Her behavior was part of the "new normal" for her and her family. She was singing, listening to music, and acting like everything was normal.

I never knew where we stood with Sarah's family. Gwyn always thought that they felt guilty that she had emerged from her coma when Bryce had not. I always thought that they were mad because their daughter would have the effects of this brain damage and her injuries for the rest of her life. I still don't know the answer to this.

Facebook Update: Wednesday 10/31/12

Sarah and her family left Japan today. They flew on a KC-135 cargo plane. They shared the plane with a newborn preemie baby.

It's Halloween and today I met with Dr. Karumai to discuss the results of yesterday's CT scan. He has now developed hydrocephalus, which is an abnormal accumulation of cerebrospinal fluid in the ventricles, or cavities, of the brain. This is causing increased intracranial pressure, so he needs a shunt surgically inserted into his brain to relieve it. However, he cannot have this surgery because his skull fractures have not yet fused and fluid is still leaking out of these cracks. The risk for infection going to his brain is stopping them from moving forward.

The Japanese surgical shunt kit and pressure pumps are a different technology than the American versions. So even if they did the surgery here in Japan, once Bryce is moved to an American hospital, the Japanese pressure pump wouldn't work.

Please pray with me that God would resolve the hydrocephalus quickly.

Love, Cathy

Life Offline

When we drove back onto base tonight, we saw a few "trick-or-treaters" walking the streets with their parents. It immediately brought back memories of Bryce and Madison, dressed up and excited as they got more than their share of Halloween candy in their pillowcases over the years. I'm starting to realize that the holidays are going to be extra tough.

NOVEMBER

Facebook Update: Thursday 11/1/12

Many of you have asked how Gwyn and I are doing, so I will take just a minute to catch you up. We stay all day at the hospital until visiting hours are over and get back on base around 8:00 p.m.

Our poor FLO is being run ragged. She does so much for us. Amazingly, she always has a kind word to offer and a smile on her face.

During the evening hours, we check our messages, try to call home, write updates on Bryce's condition, and eat dinner, which has been provided for us by caring people here in Misawa.

Occasionally, we may have to run an errand or do a couple loads of laundry. After a very full evening, we fall into bed attempting to get a good night's sleep.

This lack of rest might explain why the nurses at the hospital have been writing secret notes about Gwyn and me in Bryce's chart. We heard about these ""notes" from Dr. Wright, who is able to read some Japanese. There is concern we are wearing ourselves out. So on Monday the caring military "higher up types" semi-ordered us to take a break. We were shown a few tour options, and we chose the "Chrysanthemum Festival Day Trip" tour in Hirosaki this coming Saturday.

Trust me, it's hard for us to leave for a day, but when every medical professional is telling Gwyn and I we need to get away for our own good, we know that we need to listen. We want to be strong for Bryce, and we must recharge.

Facebook Update: Friday 11/2/12

Dr. Wright assured me that they have a plan, a contingency plan, and a few extra back-up plans that can be rolled out to meet every medical need Bryce has. The ultimate goal is to get him back on U.S. soil as quickly and safely as possible. Right now he is in no condition to be moved, but depending on too many factors to list, that can change rapidly.

One thing I wanted to pass on to my wing sisters and wing brothers, please make sure, if you can, to have a "power of attorney for medical and financial decisions," and a "living will" for your son or daughter serving in the military. Bryce and I did this together after he graduated from basic training. The military provided this service for us at no cost. Having these documents has made a horrible situation a little bit easier, and I have been able to move quickly at closing his accounts and getting his affairs in order.

Facebook Update: Saturday 11/3/12

Our day of rest in Hirosaki was wonderful. The Chrysanthemum Festival was one of the most beautiful events I have ever been to. It reminded me of the Smoky Mountains with a Japanese twist. The fall leaves were breathtaking. So glad we went.

Life Offline

Gwyn and I desperately needed this time away from the base and hospital. The tension between us had been steadily rising over the last couple of weeks, and I assumed this was one of the observations that was noted in Bryce's medical chart. It was a time of "walking on eggshells," extreme fatigue, and irritability on both sides. I had strong conflicting thoughts and feelings about having her here with me.

I love Gwyn, but by this time I wanted her to go home. Of course I was grateful to her for dropping everything and flying halfway across the world to be with me, but this just made the feelings I was having even worse. On the one hand, how could I ever say thank you enough for all her efforts and the time spent trying to help and support me? But the reality of this situation was that we seemed to be on two completely different realms when it came to interacting with Bryce, our schedules, and our individual needs. Instead of feeling like I was carrying half the load, I felt like I was carrying twice the load.

I was confused by my feelings and was too ashamed to share my honest thoughts with Gwyn. Barely able to face my own feelings, and not wanting to hurt hers, I privately asked Jackson not to issue her any new traveling orders once we left Japan. I made it clear that I wanted her to go home before our friendship became collateral damage in this already horrible situation. I knew that none of this was her fault; it was simply the shock and trauma of a parent's worst nightmare wreaking havoc in my heart and mind.

Facebook Update: Sunday 11/4/12

I sat with Bryce today just holding his hand and talking to him. I want you all to know that it feels like he is hearing me. I know he has been in a coma for twenty-three days now, but it just seems like he is there. I'm so glad the Air Force has made it possible for me to be here in Japan with him.

Facebook Update: Monday 11/5/12

Miracle Day!

Tonight, at about five-thirty, Bryce woke up, and I have several videos to prove it!

I was sitting next to him, just talking away, and one of his machines started to beep. I noticed immediately that his eyes started twitching and he looked like he was starting to wake up. I wasn't sure though, so I just kept talking to him, and his eyes started to open just a little. This time I was thinking that this might just be reflexes, so instead of reacting, I just kept talking to him. After about a minute of this twitching and eye movement I noticed he was completely still and staring at me intently.

Jackson was with me in the ICU, but on the other side of the bed, so she could not see his face. I told her, "Hey, I think he might be waking up." So she came over to my side to see for herself. She confirmed what I had been thinking and she then asked if I was videotaping this. I grabbed my cell phone video camera and began filming the next few minutes.

At this point his eyes were open and he was looking at me. As I was talking I asked him to blink. Although extremely delayed, he blinked on command, numerous times too! Then I got the nurse and told her that Bryce had been asleep twenty-four days and is now awake. She walked to the bed very slowly and pulled out a flashlight to see if there was any reaction when she flashed it in to his eyes. There must have been some because she got super excited and said, "I go call Sensei!"

Dr. Karumai came quickly. His exact words when he saw Bryce's eyes open after being closed for twenty-four days were, "This is definitely a miracle!" I was able to video his reaction on my cell phone.

Bryce woke up by himself. He is under extremely heavy sedation and unable to move. The doctors plan to slowly reduce his sedation level over the next couple of days. That will give us more information about his condition.

I consider this "our" miracle. Thank you all for your continued prayers!

Love, Cathy

Life Offline

I received this today from Madison.

"Hey Momma!

I have really wanted to see those videos of Bryce. Could you please send them to me? I want to see him blink. I want to hear the doctor say that it is a miracle. It would really mean a lot to me if you could send them.

I miss you guys so, so, so, much!

I love you Momma

Muah!

Madi"

I wanted to send her the video immediately, but I was having trouble with the big file size. I knew she was silently suffering as she worried about her big brother. She was also struggling with home, school, and life in general because of worries and missing her Momma. I prayed that God would surround her with his love and comfort.

Facebook Update: Tuesday 11/6/12

Yesterday was a true miracle! I'm praising God for the mighty work He has done!

Today Bryce slept all day and didn't wake up. This could be normal. All of the leakage of the cerebrospinal fluid seems to have completely stopped. This is a huge answer to prayer!

Dr. Karumai lowered his sedation level by twenty percent today. We did continue to see some seizure activity happening, but I don't know how much is considered typical with all he's been through.

Monday's CT scan showed worsening of his hydrocephalus, so they did another CT scan today and it was just a little worse than yesterday's. Bottom line, he needs surgery within the next week. The Air Force is making plans now to have Bryce Medevac'd out via a specialized ICU plane – an actual intensive care unit in the air. It's comforting to me knowing the Air Force is going to such incredible lengths to assure Bryce gets the proper medical care.

Love, Cathy

Chapter Five

Flight to America

Facebook Update: Wednesday 11/7/12, 5:30 a.m.

The Air Force Critical Care Air Transport Team (CCATT) will be picking up Bryce and me this afternoon. He will be having his surgery in Honolulu, Hawaii, at Tripler Army Medical Center. We will stay in Hawaii until he heals from his surgery.

Life Offline

Jackson explained to Gwyn that her military travel orders were not being renewed. She would not be traveling on with me and Bryce, but instead she would be flying home. In her desire to support me, Gwyn began insisting that she could go with me. She said her husband stood behind her and that she was willing to stay with us all the way until mid-to-late November. Basically, her husband had made it clear that he wanted her back home before Thanksgiving, but until then she had his blessing to stay the course.

This unanticipated protest put Jackson and the Air Force in a very awkward situation. There was no good reason to take away my support now, especially with Bryce remaining so critical, and everyone involved knew it. They were simply respecting my private wishes by not issuing a new set of travel orders for Gwyn.

After this development, I was pulled aside by Jackson who expressed the need for me to step up and share my concerns and wishes with Gwyn myself. "She is your best friend, after all," she protested.

I heard her loud and clear. It wasn't fair that I put the military in this situation, making them appear to be the bad guy. I had a decision to make. I could be honest with Gwyn and tell her I would like her to go home, or I could fake it and allow new travel orders to be prepared. In the end, my body decided for me. Overloaded with grief, fear, and guilt, I began to have a panic attack. Within seconds, I blurted out that I wanted Gwyn to stay with me. Jackson nodded and made it happen.

Facebook Update: Wednesday 11/7/12, 3:00 p.m.

Bryce, Gwyn, and I are all leaving for Okinawa, Japan via C-135 ICU plane. We will spend some time there, and head to Hawaii in a day or two. Gwyn has been approved to stay with me in Hawaii as Bryce continues to heal. Please pray for our safe travels, especially that Bryce will tolerate all of this.

Facebook Update: Thursday 11/8/12

We made it to Okinawa safely in the wee hours of the morning. I was completely overwhelmed by the love the Japanese doctors and nurses showed. We had arrived in the evening to make this move, and four of Bryce's day-shift nurses had been waiting for hours after their shift on their own time because they wanted to say good-bye and do whatever they could to help prepare him for this transfer, which was a lot of work.

These nurses also walked with me and Gwyn as we followed Bryce out of the hospital to the waiting ambulance, and they cried with us as we parted. It was just an overwhelming feeling of love which crossed cultures and language barriers. I am sure going to miss them. They are friends for life.

When we arrived at the airfield we were again overwhelmed by our Misawa Air Base send-off. A crowd had gathered, including all the people that had so graciously helped us over the last month with friendship, food and logistics.

On the tarmac was Bryce's AMMO family, the base Wing Commander, and the Chief of the base, along with their wives. The Wing Commander and Chief of the base each gave me one of their personal challenge coins to give to Bryce when he recovers. Their concern and care for Bryce came across loud and clear. What an amazing group of people that we have come to know and love.

Life Offline

The plane was freezing cold, so we all wore heavy coats or blankets. We were also given protective earplugs because of the loud noise. Sitting sideways in a jump seat, with cargo strapped down all around us, was a surreal experience for me.

Once we landed at Kadena Air Base, in Okinawa, Japan, the medical team took Bryce off the plane, and Gwyn and I followed behind. We were then transported to U.S. Naval Hospital Okinawa on Camp Lester. When we arrived at the military hospital, Bryce was taken in one direction to be assessed. Gwyn and I were escorted to an ICU waiting room area where we waited for several hours. Eventually, I was called into the ICU to be with Bryce. This is when I met the first American neurologist to see Bryce. He told me matter-of-factly that Bryce's injuries were catastrophic.

Facebook Update: Friday 11/9/12

Today has been the worst day I can ever remember having. I am heartbroken and praying for hope.

We met with the neurologist today, an American military doctor. I was so excited about finally getting a report that I would be able to understand. Well, it was not the report I was hoping for.

He told us that Bryce has suffered a severe diffuse axonal injury (DAI), which is similar to "shaken baby syndrome." He has severe shearing injuries in his brain and a shattered skull. He used the example of an egg that has been dropped and the shell is broken throughout.

He said his brain was like a bowl of gelatin that has been shaken back and forth. The damage is very severe. He has seen numerous cases like this and he has never seen much recovery—and typically there is no recovery at all.

Unfortunately the severe damage was on the left side of his brain where cognitive thinking is located, and also in the frontal portion of his brain, which controls his ability to concentrate as well as behave appropriately.

I was trying so hard to hold in the tears. I told him that after twenty-four days in a coma Bryce woke up, and I could show him a video of him looking at me and blinking when I asked him to.

He quickly dismissed this and said that it might have seemed that way to me, but it was all coincidence.

He then shared that when we go to Hawaii, Bryce will be having a shunt surgery in his brain which will need to drain in to his abdomen. He will also need a second surgery in his abdomen to place a PEG tube, which will be used to feed him.

The neurologist said he was not sure what the plans would be for Bryce after Hawaii. He told me Bryce would not be able to go to a traumatic brain injury rehabilitation center unless he could be an "active participant." He didn't hold much hope of that happening, and instead, believes that Bryce will be going to a nursing home. He said in six months we would know the extent of Bryce's recovery.

Hearing this blunt, frank news from an expert was devastating! I started to feel like I couldn't breathe and something was crushing me. Gwyn and I barely made it to the ICU waiting room where we both started weeping. We wanted out of Okinawa!

In the middle of all of this, we also found out Bryce's ICU flight to Hawaii had been cancelled due to an unexpected mechanical malfunction. We don't even know if we'll be able to get Bryce out of here by Saturday or Sunday.

In the midst of this mess, we called Bryce's First Sergeant in Misawa, crying out for hope and help. I knew I could count on her because she was the person with me at the hospital in

Hachinohe when Bryce woke up. She witnessed the miracle with me and I know she believes it was no coincidence. She listened to my cries and then quickly jumped into motion.

She called out the troops, literally, to come to our aid. Within minutes we had a Senior Master Sergeant from Kadena Air Force Base at our side in the ICU waiting room. He began making calls to help us with logistics, food, water, and lodging. He was so kind. He even said he was happy to help family any time. We were no longer alone in a foreign land left to freak out!

I have so much more to say, but I need to stop here for the night. We need rest and prayer. Please don't stop praying for Bryce!

Love, Cathy

Life Offline

After giving me this devastating news, the neurologist gently grabbed my hand, gave it a little squeeze, looked into my eyes, and said, "Okay? All right? Do you have any questions for me?"

I was devastated, so I just said, "No."

At this point, I was trying to stay standing. I tried to comprehend that this "American expert" who I'd been so excited to finally meet had absolutely no hope for Bryce. I instantly hated him.

Who did he think he was to act so smug and quickly dash all of our hopes? I needed to get out of there. I thought I might pass out or throw up. I couldn't really hear anymore, and I was having trouble seeing too. I was not safe here. Bryce was not safe here. I walked right out the ICU door, immediately turned right, and felt my legs buckling, as I began sobbing on the ICU patient family waiting room floor.

The whole time since Bryce's accident, outside of the first day running around screaming and panicking in my own home with Jim and Madison, I tried to hold it together. I had been brave and not overdramatic. I didn't do any of the outrageous things one would expect a mom to do in this horrible situation. But after meeting with this brain specialist, just feet away from my sweet Bryce, I lost it. I fell on the floor and cried out, "His life is ruined! What's going to happen? Everything is so horrible!"

After a few moments, I called Jim, just crying and crying. I told him what the neurologist said. I also told him that earlier in the day I read terrible comments on the Facebook page saying that it was time to pull the "#@!&*-ing" plug, that I was not facing reality, and that all the prayer warriors were enabling me to be so blankety-blank delusional.

Gwyn was sobbing uncontrollably too. I remember being really mad that Jim wasn't there. I felt like a single mom at this point. And I totally understood that Jim was home taking care of work, our home, Madison, and our pets. We would have lost everything without his sacrifice. But I still felt so pissed. I kept asking myself WHY? Why was I here by myself going through this? I didn't even think of Gwyn being with me. I felt like I was alone. I felt like Jim could do something if he was with us. Maybe they would listen to him because he is strong, and he's a veteran. Maybe they'd listen, and fix Bryce.

Bryce did not even see an American neurologist, or brain injury doctor, for 27 days. That is a long time for an active duty airman to go without being seen by a U.S. medical specialist. Ten years ago, there was an American hospital on Bryce's base in Misawa, but due to budget cuts, they closed it down and shipped out the medical staff. The 8,000 lives weren't worth it in comparison to the financial burden. As a result, if an airman has a major medical problem on base, they will put him on a C-130 and fly him to Hawaii for treatment. If he has a trauma, like Bryce did, then good luck. The outcome depends on whether or not the Japanese want to take care of him. They don't have to, and certain treatments and services can be withheld, without question, as they were in Bryce's case.

If Bryce had been shot in the head in Afghanistan or Iraq and sustained the same exact injuries, he would have been flown out immediately to a military hospital in Landstuhl, Germany, or Bethesda, Maryland, for emergency treatment. But because Bryce was serving in Japan, he didn't receive that treatment.

Financially, the military has had to make their choices, specifically which troops will get the expedited emergency medical care they need, and which troops may not be in a position to receive the same level of help. I think the military should make this information clear for all service members to review, prior to having them fill out their "wish list" for desired duty stations, so they will fully understand the extra risks involved.

Chapter Six

Angel of Intercession

It was now clear that the risk of Bryce being left in Japan had outweighed the risk of him being flown out. Something had to be done immediately or Bryce would not survive. He needed the brain shunt to help lower the pressure inside his brain before all of his brain cells died.

I was continuing to cry as I processed this devastating information in the ICU waiting room when the door opened and a man with a teenage boy entered the room. I quickly crawled forward, got up, and sat down in a chair. Gwyn got up to make room for them to sit down, and she came over and sat in a chair closer to me. I was still crying, but quietly. Gwyn and I started talking to each other about Bryce. A moment later the man looked over toward us and said, "Are you talking about the airman in Misawa who was in the accident?"

"Yes," we answered simultaneously.

"My wife, Marta, has been praying for him. It's Bryce, right?"

I was shocked and excited by his words. We were in a totally different place, feeling all alone, and this guy knows about our situation!

"Yes, Bryce is my son."

He introduced himself as Joel, and told us they were following the updates on the Facebook prayer page. Instantly my "no hope" was replaced with "new hope." I was so excited that these people were praying for Bryce. All of a sudden, we were connected to somebody!

"I'm here with my wife, Marta," he explained. "She started having chest pains and I think she's having a heart attack."

"Oh, let's pray for her," Gwyn responded. Immediately the focus was taken off of us and our misery and we had something else to concentrate on, which was a blessing.

We were overwhelmed that there were actually real live people from around the world praying for Bryce! We sure needed this boost of faith in this dark hour.

After a couple minutes, the ICU nurse came in and told Joel he could go see his wife for a few minutes. His son couldn't go with him, so he stayed in the waiting room. After a few minutes Joel returned to the waiting room and told us they were monitoring Marta's heart and everything was looking better.

"I told her I met you guys and she said 'That's why I'm here. Nothing is wrong with me.'"

After a few moments, Gwyn and I got up to go visit Bryce, but first, we snuck into Marta's private room. We introduced ourselves and she was just so giddy. "Nothing's wrong with me," she said with a grin. "I didn't have a heart attack. I'm an intercessor. I'm a prayer warrior. I've been praying for your son. Oh, I can't believe he's here. I can't wait to tell my friends!"

She was so excited to see us that an alarm on one of the machines connected to her went off. A nurse immediately came in the room to check both Marta and the machine. Thankfully, the heart rate increase was caused by her excitement and it quickly returned to normal. The nurse gave us a stern look and reminded Marta the ICU was for resting.

Marta was giggling and smiling when the nurse left her room. "My heart is perfectly fine! God wanted me here to pray over you and Bryce." She asked if she could pray for me, and of course I said, "Yes." She did, and it was the most beautiful, spirit-filled prayer ever!

She also asked permission to go pray over Bryce, later, when she could sneak out of her room. Of course I said, "Yes" again. Bryce was in the middle of the ICU, there were no doors to close for privacy. She had to wait until the middle of the night to lay hands on him and pray.

Just in case, I did add her to the visitors list so she would not get into any trouble. Can you even imagine, this sweet woman was completely fine with being in the ICU, hooked up to monitors and machines, having her blood drawn and everything else she endured, all because she felt like God blessed her with a mission to pray for us!

After receiving Marta's prayer, we went back to the waiting room and told her husband and son everything. Soon after, our new Air Force liaison arrived. He picked us up, took care of our luggage, drove us to our hotel on Kadena Air Base, and helped us check in.

Facebook Update: Friday 11/9/12, 10:45 a.m.

After a better night's sleep, I woke up ready to fight again. We got this! Bryce is in God's hands, and I trust Him to heal Bryce completely!

I wish all of you could see these videos of Bryce waking up a few days ago. They are real. His delayed blinks were not coincidences. He heard me talking to him and he knows I am here helping him to fight his way back!

Thank you all for not allowing me to give up. You are all so loved and appreciated! Today will be a great day as the Lord is in control!

Love, Cathy

Facebook Update: Friday 11/9/12, 8:00 p.m.

It looks like we are boarding an ICU flight tomorrow. We are so thankful to be heading out to Hawaii, and to be back on U.S. soil.

Please pray that Bryce does well with tomorrow's long flight. We have been told that flying is extremely hard on patients with critical injuries, and when you are in Bryce's condition, it's even more taxing.

Please pray for our safe travel.

Love, Cathy

Facebook Update: Saturday 11/10/12, 2:00 a.m.

Just wanted to let everyone know one of our local North Carolina news stations, WCNC, is doing a story on Bryce today. It will air on TV this evening, and it will also be viewable on the internet. I am set up to do a live interview via Skype in a few hours. In addition, the station sent a reporter and camera crew to our home to interview Jim.

Thank you all so much for sharing this page with your family, friends, coworkers, and churches. Now we can have even more people rallying for Bryce! I love you all so much!

Love, Cathy

Bryce, Gwyn, and I are getting ready to board a C-17 and begin our ten-hour journey to Hawaii. I can't wait to be that much closer to home.

Life Offline

Again, this plane was cold, loud, and uncomfortable as we began the long ocean flight to Hawaii. They set the calibrations in the plane to seem as though we were flying at a lower altitude than we were for Bryce's benefit. They gave us a bag lunch: a sandwich, a piece of fruit, chips, and a drink. It was nice to have this meal. I had not slept the night before and now I could hardly keep my eyes open. Gwyn had slept soundly, so she tucked me in with blankets and then stayed awake watching Bryce through the entire flight as I was gently rocked to sleep.

Facebook Update: Friday 11/10/12, 4:00 a.m. EST.

We have just landed on American soil in Hawaii. The medical flight was once again amazing. We landed at Hickam AFB and took a 20-minute ride to Tripler Army Medical Center.

Life Offline

They brought Bryce to the hospital, but they wouldn't allow us to go with him. Bryce had to be thoroughly examined by the new attending physicians and we couldn't be there for any of that.

They dropped Gwyn and me off in the front lobby of the Army hospital so we could meet with an Air Force Liaison and get checked into our hotel. We pulled our carry-on luggage down the long hallway to the Military Liaisons' offices, but since it was Veteran's Day weekend, they were away enjoying the holiday.

So after all that waiting, here we were waiting again.

It all seemed eerily similar to our non-welcome in Okinawa, and we didn't know where to turn. We were on a military base, but I had no military ID. We had no food, no lodging, no FLO, no car—basically we had no support. And my Bryce had been whisked away to the ICU. Welcome to America!

My crying meltdown quickly ensued.

I called Jim, rambling about our situation and bawling hysterically. We were so tired, hungry, and dirty from the flight. We just sat on the floor in a hospital hallway, while I talked to Jim. We decided I should call General Wilfong, a friend of Bryce's from our hometown of Monroe, North Carolina. He was now a commercial pilot with US Airways but was still in the Air Force National Guard.

I called him crying, explained our situation, and told him that we were hungry and had nowhere to go. He was so kind, and he seemed confused that there was no one there to pick us up and get us situated. He said he would make some phone calls and try to get us some help. He was getting ready to board a plane out of the country, so he warned it could take some time.

General Wilfong was actually able to get in touch with someone associated with the top brass on base, and it wasn't long before we had new friends in high places. The Base Commander was informed of our plight, and he was on it immediately. Within a short time, military personnel called me from Pearl Harbor saying help was on the way.

Someone in uniform showed up, opened the hospital military liaison office, and gave us the rest of our luggage that had been locked up inside. Then we were driven to a hotel near the hospital to check in and finally rest for a few minutes. As soon as I entered my room, I received a message from Theresa Johnson, who runs the Tripler Fisher House. (A Fisher House is a free, or low cost, lodging facility for veteran and military families to stay in while loved ones receive treatment in a military hospital or medical center.) She said she had been following Bryce's journey on Facebook and had been praying for him. She said she had a room waiting for us.

I called and told her that we had already checked in to the hotel. She said, "No problem. Just go check out and I'll send someone to come pick you up."

Gwyn was so exhausted from staying up through the flight. She immediately took a shower when we arrived at the hotel, and after her shower she literally crawled in to bed and cried herself to sleep. Once in bed, it was clear she was not going anywhere. I explained the situation to the hotel manager, and he decided to allow us to check out early and only charged us for one night. This allowed Gwyn to stay put and get some much-needed sleep.

I went alone to the beautiful Fisher House. It was a lovely home setting with a living room, kitchen, dining room, washer and dryer, and a beautiful view from the top of a hill in Honolulu. After a quick tour and orientation on house rules and expectations, I left for the hospital to check on Bryce.

Tripler Army Medical Center is fantastic. The large, pink hospital is built into a mountainside, and there are breathtaking views everywhere you look. The front faces the Pacific Ocean and beaches, and the backside faces the Moanalua Ridge. Bryce has a big window in his ICU room, and I hope one day he will be able to appreciate the superb beauty outside.

Specific prayer requests:

1. For Bryce to be miraculously healed.

2. For a great report from the neurology team tomorrow.

3. For Bryce to wake up and recognize me again.

Thank you so much for pressing on with us! Something wonderful will come from all of this!

Love, Cathy

Life Offline

Not long after Gwyn and I arrived in Hawaii, I received this very sweet note from Yuko.

"Cathy,

Did you put safety in Hawaii? Have you determined the day of the surgery of "baby Bryce?" I'm worried because it was causing convulsion on the day of departure.

And how are you and Gwyn?

Bryce was suddenly depart, there is no surprise that many ICU staff! Bryce was gone, I'm feeling a little empty. (; _ ;)/~~

And I was nice to meet you heart is wide and funny friend. o(*∩−∩*)o

I love your book♪ It became the days unforgettable!

I hope you and Bryce meet the family soon.

Yuko"

By "book" she was referring to the prayer page. Yuko almost always used a Japanese-to-English translation book to converse with me. Without realizing it, she made my mostly tough and serious days a little happier; because I enjoyed the funny ways some of the Japanese words would translate into English. I was honored that she tried so hard to talk to me. After reading her note, I realized how blessed I was to have met her, and I sure missed my new forever friend!

Today we met an amazing neurosurgeon! Not only is he brilliant, he is also kind. He listened to me and answered all of my answerable questions. He was realistic with me and even shared that he doesn't know today what the future holds for Bryce.

He taught me about the brain—what is normal and abnormal—and shared a road map of Bryce's treatment, and hopefully his recovery. This truly gave me renewed strength and hope.

What we see today may not be Bryce's final outcome. Every brain injury is unique. As a matter of fact, he will be re-evaluated continuously throughout his recovery. We are in the very early stages; he is only one month out. So we have plenty of time to pray.

I sure do appreciate you praying and believing for Bryce's full recovery!

Love, Cathy

Life Offline

This neurosurgeon was so different than the neurologist I met in Okinawa. He was straightforward, but he didn't leave us without any hope. I was so thankful to be able to talk to him about Bryce.

One of my Facebook wing sisters called her mom and stepdad in Hawaii, and asked if they could help us. Her stepfather, Eric Weilenmen—the Captain of the U.S.S. *Port Royal*, a Navy Ticonderoga-class guided missile cruiser, whose homeport is in Pearl Harbor—dropped whatever he was doing and came right over to the hospital. We made introductions and then he drove us to a military supermarket, also known as the commissary, so we could buy some food.

I was so thankful for this kind man. Here he was, the captain of a ship, a military bigwig, and I was just a mom. Yet he treated us like we were the special ones. He changed our lives that day and made a seemingly hopeless situation one that could be survived.

In time, we received fresh military orders; a base ID, which allowed me into the commissary to purchase groceries; and a new FLO, who introduced us to a chain of support personnel and a few families on base.

Some of these families arranged for folks to cook homemade hot meals and have them delivered to us at the hospital each day. This was over and above anything we ever expected to happen. We now had everything we needed. Instead of worrying about our own needs, we could now spend all of our time loving on Bryce and praying for his recovery.

Facebook Update: Monday 11/12/12

If you have ever wondered whether prayer changes your circumstances, let me assure you, it does.

Last night I asked you to please pray for Bryce because he was so sick, and he just looked miserable. I received a lot of "likes" and encouraging comments on Facebook, so I know that many people did pray for him.

When I went to see him this morning, he looked great! His test for pneumonia was negative.

Today was the first day since the accident that Bryce actually looked like his old self.

All of the issues from yesterday just seemed to resolve. If he continues to do well tonight he will be able to have his much-needed surgery tomorrow. They plan to re-evaluate him in the morning. Thank you so much for praying with me and helping to change Bryce's circumstances!

Facebook Update: Tuesday 11/13/12

The neurosurgeon said Bryce came through the surgery just fine. We will be able to see him soon. Thank you for your continued prayers for Bryce!

Love, Cathy

Life Offline

I received this encouragement on the prayer page:

"Cathy,

Praying every day for all of you. Can't imagine how difficult it must be for Jim and Madi as well so they are in my prayers too. I'm praising the Lord for healing Bryce so he could have the surgery. May Bryce get stronger every day.

Love you.

Janet"

I was so touched when I read this! I knew I was not alone. It was comforting to know I was surrounded by the Lord God and many caring prayer warriors!

Facebook Update: Wednesday 11/14/12

Bryce is doing fairly well after his surgery. His blood pressure and heart rate rose a few times today most likely due to pain.

Please say a special prayer tonight for Bryce to not have any more pain, for his entire body to be able to relax and have a good, productive rest, and for the pressures in his head and brain to lessen.

Gwyn will be leaving to go back home to her family soon. We promised her husband she would be home in time for Thanksgiving, and thanks to the Air Force, it will happen! Thank you so much, Tom Dailey, for allowing your wonderful and supportive wife to come to Japan, and Hawaii, to help support me for the last month! I don't think I would have made it through all of this without her constantly pointing me to the Lord, reading God's Word, and praying all hours. God bless you Gwyn Dailey!

Jim and Madison were planning to come to Hawaii to see Bryce the week of November 21st. As we were finalizing their travel arrangements, we were told Bryce would most likely be moving to another facility on November 16th. Because of this new information, we had to cancel their trip.

Unfortunately, after it was canceled, Bryce's move was also called off. I am disappointed. I wanted Jim and Madison to finally be able to spend time with Bryce, especially during Thanksgiving. Now, that won't be able to happen.

There are new tentative plans to move Bryce after Thanksgiving, or possibly the following week. With all of these plans up in the air, I must stay positive and continue to be patient. Honestly, I am still so grateful that we even have Bryce!

Love, Cathy

Life Offline

Before Bryce could be transferred to another hospital or facility, a doctor there would have to accept Bryce. We could not find a facility that wanted to accept a person in a vegetative state who might not be able to be an active participant. So trying to make plans for Bryce and our family was very frustrating.

Jim likes to make a plan and then work his plan. This was impossible in our current situation with Bryce. Everything was up in the air. We would have a plan, then it would be cancelled and we'd have no plan. Then a new plan would be made, and then canceled again. All of this indecisiveness wreaked havoc on our family. We were all affected—frustration, anger, apathy, depression, isolation, blame! REPEAT, REPEAT, REPEAT.

Jim wanted to see Bryce for himself because he felt he wasn't receiving answers to important questions. But once again, it was "hurry up and wait."

The reality of how life instantly changed for our entire family was starting to set in. Jim and I were barely talking at all anymore. When we did talk, it was in the form of angry emails and text messages. The frustration level was at an all-time high.

Even though Bryce's horrific injuries put his life into a holding pattern, regular life had to continue at home. Chores needed to be done. Jim's employer expected productivity and profit. Madison had school and homework. Pile on top of that a lot of stress, frustration, grief, and worry—with me in Hawaii, unable to help with anything at home.

I felt terrible knowing Jim and Madison were having such a tough time and I couldn't help them work it out. I had always been the one in our family to make sure everything was running smoothly. I took care of the cooking, grocery shopping, paying the bills, and of course, the creating and handing out of chores and honey-do-lists for everyone. We were all outside of our comfort zones and praying for a miracle!

Chapter Seven

Thanksgiving by Faith

Facebook Update: Thursday 11/15/12, 9:45 a.m.

New scans show that the ventricles in Bryce's brain do not seem to be getting any smaller, and they do not appear to be draining the cerebrospinal fluid. This much-needed draining is why they put the shunt in to begin with, so the neurosurgeon is doing a procedure to try and find out why. He's checking the pressure in Bryce brain, the plumbing inside his head, and all throughout the inside of the shunt. Please pray for Bryce to be comforted and protected during this procedure.

Thank you!

Love, Cathy

Facebook Update: Thursday 11/15/12, 11:30 a.m.

The neurosurgeon is done with the procedure. Bryce will be going down for more scans in a bit. Thank you for all the prayers being said on his behalf! I believe prayer moves mountains!

This afternoon's new scans of Bryce's brain were inconclusive, so the neurosurgeon and his team took Bryce to nuclear medicine and did a contrast scan. They were finally able to get the answers they were looking for.

1. Bryce's shunt, pump, and hardware are working perfectly.

2. Bryce's ventricles inside his brain are super full, there is a lot of pressure, and they need to turn up the flow switch to drain more of the cerebrospinal fluid. We will now wait for a new scan tomorrow to see if there is any difference.

Life Offline

I met with the hospital social worker. After going over all the latest details of Bryce's condition and our situation, she looked me in the eye and said it was important that we get away from the hospital for a while to do something fun to rejuvenate. She said she had two tickets for Gwyn and me to go to a luau. I was pretty conflicted about the idea. I didn't want to leave Bryce in the hospital while I went off to have fun at a luau.

In the end, I saw the wisdom of allowing myself some time for recreation. The luau experience was actually amazing, and both Gwyn and I enjoyed it. At the same time, I felt ashamed for going. It seemed wrong to pretend, even for just a few hours, that everything was normal. I didn't even know if Bryce was going to live or die, and I didn't want to be off at some party if he passed away.

Another day, we went to a mall so we could buy touristy-type gifts for our families. We were in Hawaii and might not ever have the opportunity to come back again, so I wanted to bring a little bit of the experience home with me. Gwyn and I bought matching wind chimes. They would be a reminder of all we had gone through together on this journey as best friends.

Facebook Update: Friday 11/16/12

Today we learned that the swelling in his ventricles was a little smaller than the scans from yesterday. This is great news! The shunt is doing its job, and the extra pressures inside his brain should be lessening.

Most of you know Bryce opened his eyes on November 5th for the first time since his accident. That was the day I videotaped him blinking for me, albeit delayed, when I asked him to. The following day, November 6th, he did not open his eyes at all. On November 7th, he did open his eyes, but this time he had a "no one home" look about him.

The neurosurgeon told me that he was still in a coma, and that sometimes people in comas will still open and close their eyes throughout the day, even though they are not actually awake. So, even though he looks awake at times, just staring straight ahead, he is still comatose. They say Bryce is at the border, trying to wake up, but just not there yet.

Yesterday, I was talking to Bryce, and sticking my face just a few inches from his, and all of a sudden it seemed to me that his "eye stare" changed, and he connected with me.

I instantly felt his eyes look in to mine, and I talked to him, telling him that I see him, and that I know he can see me. It was so cool. Unfortunately, there were no doctors there to witness what I saw.

Today it happened again, repeatedly. I just know my son is trying hard to connect with me. I was even able to move a little from right to left, and left to right, and he was able to keep his eyes locked onto mine as I moved. Of course the doctors didn't see this today, but a couple of the nurses did, as did Gwyn! This is more great news!

It appears that as the pressures are beginning to come down inside Bryce's brain, he is starting to wake up a little. I am so excited about this! I am thanking Jesus for this miracle, and believing for more to come!

Thank you for all the prayers and for believing that God is our healer! Please don't stop now! I love knowing the masses are lifting Bryce up throughout the day. I am expecting great things!

Love, Cathy

Facebook Update: Saturday 11/17/12

Every couple of hours Bryce starts to tense up, sweat, shake, and his heart rate starts climbing, eventually so high that it sets off the alarm. The nurses always come to the rescue with a little shot of something to help ease whatever is happening to him and within seconds his body completely relaxes.

Please specifically pray for Bryce to remain infection free, for the swelling and extra cerebrospinal fluid in his brain to return to normal, and for his brain to start making new, amazing connections, so he will someday be fully restored!

For my NC friends: I did an interview with our local newspaper, the "Enquirer Journal," earlier this week, and they will be featuring Bryce in Sunday's paper.

Sure do love and appreciate everyone that is praying for Bryce!

Love, Cathy

Life Offline

The medical team had slowly taken the ventilator off Bryce, as his body was learning how to breathe again. So they started being able to turn down the ventilator some, and he would do okay. Then they turned it down a little more, and he would struggle a little, so they would turn it back up some. This was a whole process. They slowly weaned him off over the course of several days. Then, on November 17, they were finally able to move this huge ventilator completely out of his ICU room.

I was so happy about this development, but at the same time, I was completely floored. I guess I never realized he could be completely free from life support and still not wake up. It hit me that we missed the part where he was supposed to wake up.

I always thought that someone in a coma is asleep, doesn't know anything, and is on a ventilator. What do you mean his body learned to breathe again, but his brain is not getting better? This really scared me.

I never thought I was going to be gone even a month. I thought that like Sarah, Bryce would wake up and we'd be going home. We would find a reputable rehabilitation place near our house, and it would be good and manageable. We'd come through this together, and Bryce would be fine.

And now he wasn't waking up and the ventilator was off. During this process, I learned that our bodies have primal instincts. If you place a bottle in the mouth of a newborn baby, they're not thinking, "Oh, it's my bottle." They just automatically start sucking. Well after some time in a coma, a person begins to have these automatic autonomic functions, things like eyes opening and closing, yawning, or sleep and waking patterns.

After roughly thirty days of an eyes-closed coma, it is not uncommon for the body to go into a new state, known as a vegetative coma vigil. The eyes may open and close, but the patient doesn't know who they are, or that they even exist.

People who are brain dead have no brain waves. Bryce still had brain waves at this point. So he was not brain dead. Just catastrophically brain injured. So now I wondered, where's Bryce? And who is this laying here? It was just a horrible feeling.

Facebook Update: Sunday 11/18/12

Praise God! More good news to share!

First, Bryce is now breathing without any assistance from the ventilator. He is still receiving forty percent oxygen through his trachea collar, but he is ventilating all on his own. This is fantastic news!

Second, Jim and Madison will be able to come
here for a few days during Thanksgiving weekend
after all! I hope it will be healing for Bryce
to hear their voices and have them close by.

Life Offline

I did a local interview with our Monroe, North Carolina,
newspaper where I told them all about Bryce and how people
from our hometown were helping by bringing meals to Jim and
Madison and organizing prayer vigils.

I also told them that Gwyn was with me and about all she was
doing to help me. Gwyn heard everything I said in the interview.
Then when the article came out, the local paper didn't reference
Gwyn at all. When he heard about it, Gwyn's husband got really
offended. He felt slighted because he was taking care of their
home and chores while she was supporting me, and he wanted
recognition for that. It caused a huge grievance between all of us.

After her husband said these things, Gwyn got angry with him,
and started crying. Later, she came and met me at the hospital
and shared their conversation with me. Then I started crying.
Gwyn told me she was mad at him for what he said. "I know it's
not right," she said through her tears.

"Gwyn, does your husband know what you told me the very first
day you arrived in Japan?" I asked in frustration. I reminded her
of the two things she promised me:

"There is nothing you can do or say through this trauma with
Bryce that will push me away or make me not love you." Gwyn
declared after she arrived. "I'm extending full grace because I can't
imagine this nightmare. I know you, Cathy, because you're my best
friend. I know you're a runner. And I just want you to know, you
can't run from me, because I'll always be here for you."

"Wow, thank God," I had responded. This made me feel safe. I started crying and gave her a hug.

"We have two completely different personalities," she added. "You can be right up front and talk in a group of people, and you're comfortable having a thousand friends. I'm more of a background person. You are here for Bryce, and I am here for you. I don't want to be in the limelight. I'm behind you, and I just want you to feel safe with that."

So later, when I was typing my updates, I thought of how Gwyn had been reading *Heaven is for Real* out loud to Bryce and me every day. I thought I really should give her credit for that. But then I remembered that Gwyn didn't want to be in the limelight, and I respected that. So I didn't mention her by name very often in my updates. I thought it was so amazing that she was willing to do this for me. I had my own little safe friend who was helping me behind the scenes, and that was very special.

I was embarrassed and offended when her husband got angry. He was mad he had to do the laundry. He was angry he had a teenager at home to take care of and his wife was with me. He wanted to know why I wasn't thanking her, or him, for their sacrifice.

I'm sure it was the heavy toll of stress that caused his outburst and not me personally, but I didn't think about that. Instead I picked up this offense, ran with it, and then I suddenly felt very unsafe. He didn't know that I had not even wanted Gwyn to be in Hawaii with me and already felt like things were a lot worse having her here. She didn't know how I was really feeling either, because I wasn't being honest with her.

I often felt like she did whatever she needed to do for Gwyn first. This situation was so hard, and so horrible, and we each kicked in to survivor mode. It wasn't that she purposefully tried to be mean or cause me harm. That wasn't it at all. I didn't set out to hurt her either. It didn't matter though. The tension between us continued to climb anyway. We were both way out of our comfort zones and without much control of anything. Add to this that we are both grown women who are a tad on the controlling side... and BOOM! Even our bodies reacted to the stress differently. At the end of each emotionally demanding day, she would collapse, falling asleep hours before me. My body reacted differently under the stress, and I would lay awake and alone for hours.

But the problem was that I didn't feel supported by her anymore—and that was the whole reason she was there. Instead, I felt very much alone, like I had to worry about her plans, wishes, and needs on top of everything else. It was an awful time.

Then there was all the stupid stuff that bothered me, like her touching Bryce last when we'd leave the hospital or when she stepped in front of me when the doctors or nurses spoke to me. She would ask the doctors questions before I could ask them. As a result, they would look at her and dialogue with her instead of with me. This happened on numerous occasions. I know Gwyn was trying to help me by doing this, but it just made me feel worse.

I felt stupid to call her out on these things, until they escalated to the point of me almost freaking out. Then I would just bowl her over with a bunch of words spoken as quickly as I could with great force so I could finally get her to stop and listen to me. I'm sure I looked foolish when I did this. I was just so desperate to not have problems with her, and sometimes I couldn't keep my thoughts to myself.

I felt like she was dead weight. She was a burden. It wasn't her fault, but it happened a lot. She would say, "Oh my stomach hurts. I'm tired. I need to buy souvenirs for my kids. I'm not feeling well. I need to go to the store and get some of this." It felt like she was fighting for control of our time, control of Bryce's doctors and nurses, control of me—control of anything. And it didn't work out that well for her, or for me.

I just wanted to sit with Bryce. I just wanted to see him wake up. I could not handle her taking over. And she always had a good reason why she wouldn't follow my simple rules. "I just wanted to make sure you didn't forget to ask the doctor what we were talking about earlier."

While this was a very tense time, looking back now, I know nothing was intentional. She loved Bryce too.

Facebook Update: Monday 11/19/12

Bryce had another CT scan today. His ventricles looked exactly the same, so the neurosurgeon adjusted his shunt. Hopefully the ventricles will start draining the extra cerebrospinal fluid ASAP and the extra pressure in his brain will also lessen.

Gwyn will be leaving for home tomorrow morning. Please pray for her safe travels, and that she would be blessed abundantly in every way. She is an amazing person, and I am blessed to have had her by my side the last five weeks! Thank you, Tom Dailey, for sharing your wife with me and Bryce!

Thank you for caring and praying!

Love, Cathy

Life Offline

An Air Force casualty liaison from Randolph Air Force Base in Texas diligently worked with Gwyn over the phone to process new travel orders and flights to get her home safely.

"I got my orders today," she said one night as we were getting ready for bed. "I fly out on November 20."

"Okay," I said, acting excited for her, like all was well between us. "I hope you don't mind that I won't be going to the airport with you."

"No, no, no," she answered. "It's fine. Stay with Bryce."

We both lay down in our beds to go to sleep. Then a few minutes later, she started crying and shaking. "This has been the hardest thing I've ever done," she said through her tears. Obviously, she was upset.

I was upset too, but I was also numb. I didn't cry. I held it all in. I was thinking to myself, "I cannot carry my weight, and her weight, one more day. She can't help or support me here in Hawaii. She has pushed herself beyond the maximum amount of what she was able to give."

I should have given her grace, but I had none to give. All I could think of at the time—the bottom line for me—was that she was sent by the Air Force to support me as I cared for Bryce. At some point, we both lost sight of that mission. I was conflicted because Gwyn had been my friend for years, and I know she tried to be supportive. But my focus had to be Bryce; it could not be Gwyn.

Trauma changes everything. It would take a miracle to fully recover our friendship after these hurtful and confusing times.

I received this note from one of the prayer warriors on the Facebook page, which helped me work through some of my feelings of Gwyn leaving:

"Father, I am so excited with the news that Cathy shared this morning about Bryce's healing. It astounds me how in the midst of all the things in this world that you can focus so much on this one man and hear our prayers. Father, we are awaiting for the news of that COMA HUG.

I pray you continue to cause the swelling to decrease. I pray that you continue to give Cathy the signs that things are improving. I am praying that you continue to lift Cathy up as she stays beside her son and waits for the day she can see him fully awake and recovered.

As Gwyn leaves Hawaii I pray Father that you place someone next to Cathy that will be her strength when she feels weak—someone who will point her to you when she is losing her direction. Give her someone that she can connect with that will help carry her until the next move.

I pray this in Jesus' precious name.

Sandy"

This prayer truly touched my heart! It was exactly what I needed at that difficult moment.

There have been no significant changes in Bryce. He is opening and closing his eyes, yawning occasionally, and doing a few other — automatic reflex" type things. He did have a scary situation happen this afternoon when his feeding tube somehow coiled up inside the back of his throat, causing the liquid they were feeding him to also fill up in his throat. He started choking and aspirating some of his liquid food into his lungs. I was with him when it happened, and when I yelled for help, about six people came rushing in. A chest x-ray confirmed the aspiration, so they will be watching him even closer for the next day or two. A new feeding tube was placed.

I wish I could wake him up, hug him, and bring him home with me today. I can't. I will try to be patient through the process. Today I am thankful for another day with him. We all know that tomorrow is not promised to anyone, and every day of life is a precious gift from God.

Jim and Madison will arrive here in Hawaii on Thanksgiving Day. I'm so thankful this is happening, and I can't wait to have some "family time!" The last time the four of us were together was when we took Bryce to the Charlotte Douglas International Airport, and hung out for a couple of hours at the USO, before he left for Misawa Air Force Base. Even though that was just last February, today that seems like a long, long time ago.

Life Offline

Bryce's social worker has been calling hospitals and rehabilitation facilities looking for a "next step" program. After several "no's" she finally received a "yes" from Dr. Pai at the Hunter Holmes McGuire Polytrauma Unit in Richmond, Virginia. We later learned that Dr. Pai is one of the most respected doctors in the country when it comes to brain trauma, emerging, and rehabilitation.

It was so encouraging to see in writing that Bryce was accepted into their ninety-day Emerging Consciousness Program instead of having to place him in a nursing home.

"You've got one last chance here to see if he wakes up," the social worker explained, "and if not, then we will find a nursing home for him."

Facebook Update: Wednesday 11/21/12

Happy Thanksgiving! I wish you all a beautiful, peaceful, and love-filled holiday.

Thank you for caring about our son, for encouraging our family, and most importantly for faithfully praying for Bryce. What a blessing you are!

Today, when the neurosurgeon examined Bryce, he told me that he noticed an improvement. Specifically, he noticed Bryce's response to pain had gotten better, and his reflexes were a little more brisk. When the doctor forcefully pinched Bryce in the upper right chest, Bryce lifted his right arm a little quicker. Bryce also tried pushing the doctor's hand away. He then did the same thing when he was pinched on the left. This is such great news!

Love, Cathy

Life Offline

I stayed at the hospital all day, and late into the night. Then I would go to the Fisher House to write my prayer page update. I would read it several times to make sure that it was right, hit the send button, and then just turn everything off. Then I would just zone, not wanting to talk to anyone. It was a chore to pick up the phone and go through all of it again with Jim and Madison. For me, Facebook was something that helped me to survive, which is a horrible thing to say.

Facebook became almost the only way I talked to Madison for several months.

Facebook Update: Thursday 11/22/12

I have a new friend. His name is Sam. We just spent some great quality time talking about Bryce. He is practically a neighbor since he is from Spartanburg, South Carolina. He assured me he is praying for Bryce to get better.

My new friend Sam is a Four Star Admiral and also the Commander of the Pacific Theatre. I don't know all the ranks, but I do know he is the "big guy." It's wonderful that he genuinely cares about the little people like us.

Love, Cathy

Life Offline

It was incredible that Admiral Samuel J. Locklear chose to share his Thanksgiving Day with the families at the Fisher House. He walked into the large kitchen, and with a wide smile he introduced himself. He was so kind. At first, I had no idea what an honor it was to meet him. As far as I knew, he was a Navy liaison stopping in for a routine visit. He prayed a blessing over the homemade turkey meal and then served each of us a plate of the mouthwatering food in the dining area. He was a friendly man and took time to get to know each of us. When it was my turn to visit with him, I asked him about all the cool stars on his collar, specifically asking him how much longer until he got to be a general. He roared with laughter, actually everyone within earshot did. I was serious though; being an Air Force mom, I had no idea how the Navy rank and stars functioned. Trying to impress him, I shared that I had a friend who actually knows the Four-Star General on base in Pearl Harbor. He seemed impressed, and at the same time, he chuckled. Thinking I was being encouraging, I asked him again how many more years he had to serve to be a general someday. This time he realized I had no idea he was the top brass, so he said, "You know the Four-Star Air Force General you mentioned?"

"Yes" I replied.

"Well he works for me."

Poor guy, I thought he must be confused. He was Navy, and the General I had been referring to was Air Force. I kindly explained the difference to him. He burst out laughing again. Over the next minute, he explained that the Air Force General in Hawaii reported to him. He went on to explain that he, a Navy guy, was in charge of all the military troops serving in South Korea, Japan, and Hawaii, and that all of the different military branch leaders in each of those areas worked for him. WOW! I had no idea that's how the military branches operated or that they even worked together. I was instantly and simultaneously, impressed and embarrassed. He enjoyed every minute of our conversation, and told me from now on I could call him "Sam." We were friends after all, and he reminded me that he cares about Bryce and said if I ever needed his help, I could call on him.

This had to be the huge favor of God! I will never forget his kindness. He clearly went out of his way to offer me his personal support.

After our meal and visit, I walked to the hospital to check on Bryce. I told him today was Thanksgiving and also the day Dad and Madi were coming to see him.

Facebook Update: Thursday 11/22/12

Today is a great day! Our family is together again, and I am thankful! Jim and Madison arrived in the ICU a little before 3:00 p.m. It was the first time since the accident they were able to lay eyes on, talk to, touch, and care for Bryce in their own precious ways. It was a special time for all of us.

Jim felt relieved to see Bryce. He immediately had a sense of "Okay, we got this! Things are going to be okay." You see, like Bryce, he is a strong AMMO man, and he is ready and willing to do whatever it takes to stay strong, lead our family, and help his son beat this.

Madison had a much harder time. It clearly broke her heart to see her big brother in his condition, and it was evident that it also scared her. At first, she wouldn't approach the side of his bed. Then once she was able to get alongside him, she couldn't speak. She was broken, overwhelmed with grief and sadness, and it took her a while to come to grips that regardless of the injuries this is still our Bryce in that bed. She eventually did. She is compassionate and I love her tender heart.

Bryce's amazing neurosurgeon came in on his Thanksgiving holiday so he could talk to Jim and Madison about Bryce. He wanted to make sure they both had a good understanding of his injuries. He answered all of our questions as best he could.

Amazingly enough, one of the last things he told us was that Bryce is now in a "semi-sleep-state" or a semi-conscious state, and is trying to wake up. He said his brain injuries are very bad, but quickly reminded us that he survived and that he is now showing improvement.

Praise God for a wonderful report on this Thanksgiving Day! Please don't stop praying and believing for a complete miracle healing for our, and your, Bryce!

Love, Cathy

Life Offline

I couldn't wait for this to happen. I wanted to know if Jim could tell if Bryce would live or die. When he looks at people, Jim sometimes sees a light around them, and there have been times when Jim could tell if someone was going to die soon. There was one instance when Jim came home and told me that someone at work, who was perfectly healthy, was going to die within a week. I was shocked when only a few days later this man was killed in an accident.

This has happened several times since I've known Jim. So when they arrived I was no longer looking at Bryce, I was watching Jim, seeing what kind of look he had on his face.

"What do you see? What do you see?"

"He still has a light," he replied.

"So is he going to be okay?"

"I think he will be okay. His light is really dim, but I still see light."

I was so excited! I knew everything was going to be okay after Jim saw Bryce.

After several minutes waiting in the hallway, Madison finally got the courage to come into the room. She was still scared and she would not go near him. Bryce had just had brain surgery, so his head was shaved and he had stitches and staples all over the place. He looked like Frankenstein, so I could understand Madison being upset.

I tried to be a good parent, like when a kid doesn't want to do something they need to do and so you push them. I was trying to manipulate her into going and hugging him. I knew that once she did, she would be fine. "This is your brother," I said. "This is Bryce. Madi, get over here." But this didn't work, and it just made things ten times worse.

I pushed her over to him. She was standing right next to his bed, and she looked like she was going to throw up. It was so much pressure. It was awful.

Jim was mad at her, and Madison was mad at him, and I was mad at her, and Jim was mad at me. And then someone would walk in and ask, "How is the Powers family doing?" And we'd say, "Good, good, good. Thank you for asking."

I got so upset at Jim and Madison. After being there for only two hours, they wanted to leave to go get something to eat! I couldn't help thinking, "What kind of people are they?"

But the doctors were telling Jim, "Get her out of here. She shouldn't be here this much." I didn't know this, so I thought Jim was being insensitive to Bryce.

So I was getting mad at them, thinking, "Don't they love Bryce?" And they were thinking, "We're trying to take care of you."

The doctor had come in and given us all the information that we needed on Bryce's condition. Jim knew that nothing was going to change for the next couple of hours.

"Let's go get some dinner," he prodded. "Let's get you out of here."

But I yelled at him, "What are you doing? My son's dying."

"Who said he is dying?" Jim answered. "You need a break from this place. Let's go eat."

Later, I wrote on Facebook, "Jim and Madi were finally able to see Bryce, and the Powers Family is all together again...." But behind the scenes, I was saying to God, "Just kill us all."

After all the anticipation of Jim and Madison coming to visit, their presence just added to my overwhelming stress, just as Gwyn had done. After only a few hours, I couldn't wait for them to leave. I wanted them gone so I could get back to helping Bryce heal.

On Friday, Eric Weilenman, who has been absolutely wonderful and a lifesaver for me since I arrived in Hawaii, came by the hospital to check on Bryce and also to meet Jim and Madison. We had a great visit. He surprised us by presenting our family with a flag that was flown on the U.S.S. *Port Royal* for a day especially for Bryce and a beautiful color photo of the ship that was signed by his crew. I'll never forget Eric and his wife Wanda for their help!

Whew! The last two days have been a whirlwind here.

Bryce is continuing to rest for the most part, but has had many autonomic brain storms, which are essentially a nonstop shaking, mixed with a drenching sweat, and sometimes fevers that last for hours on end. This is all part of his brain injury. I have no idea how long this will continue for him. Hopefully, in time, they will pass.

Jim and Madison are in the air now, on their way back home. It was so great to have them here for a couple of days! We learned a lot about patient care, and worked hard together, so we can all help Bryce get better.

Life Offline

Jim and Madison actually left for the airport not speaking to each other. To be perfectly honest, it was one of the worst, and most stressful, holidays we have ever had. We were on each other's nerves the entire time.

I was way too bossy when it came to the rules of how to best care for Bryce, since I was the only one who had been with him. I was secretly mad that they hadn't been with us. I completely understood all the reasons why they couldn't be, but I still had the angry feelings in my heart.

Jim told me he was extremely angry with me for seeming to always have my phone off or not calling him back quickly enough after his calls. I tried to remind him that Bryce is in the ICU and no phones are allowed, but that just made him more upset. I told him that he should read my Facebook prayer page updates for a better understanding of what's happening with Bryce. He said he flat out refused to read anything on Facebook, including my updates.

Madison was afraid to get too close to Bryce. I yelled at her and tried to guilt her into getting closer to him. I scolded her, telling her to talk to him and show him some love.

What a nightmare! I am ashamed to say it, but I was actually glad they were going home. I was tired of the crying and fighting. We all needed a miracle, not just Bryce.

Chapter Eight

To the Mainland

I had remained by Bryce's side from the time I arrived, even on his ICU flights from Japan to Hawaii. But after he was accepted to the Richmond VA hospital, the case worker told me I would have to take a separate commercial flight to Virginia or home to North Carolina so I could get some rest. They were trying to encourage me to go home, spend some time with the family, and then drive up to Richmond at a later date. Of course, this made me very upset. "No, no, no!" I told them, "I have been with Bryce the whole time and I'm not leaving his side."

"Well, we don't really do that," the case worker explained. "We're going to have to try to get him on a military flight, but you won't be able to travel with him."

"I don't care," I dug in my heels. "I'm not leaving without my son." It was basically a standoff.

Once again I was in despair over the situation. Then suddenly a doctor from the emergency department visited me out of the blue. "My wife is one of Bryce's nurses, and she has been telling me about your situation. I'm a member of the CCATT flight team. If it's okay with you, I would like to submit paperwork asking the military to give me a plane to transport Bryce to Richmond as soon as possible. This will allow you to travel with Bryce."

I was blown away.

The emergency department doctor was able to get Bryce's CCATT paperwork approved, and it was not any kind of a normal, typical operation. This was a special flight they put together to meet Bryce's critical needs. Once again, God provided in a special way—and it was very nice of the Air Force to pay to transport me and Bryce together.

Facebook Update: Saturday 11/24/12

It's official, tonight is our last night in Hawaii. Bryce and I leave for the Richmond, Virginia, Polytrauma Center tomorrow afternoon. We will be traveling to the East Coast via an Air Force KC-135 ICU plane. This will be our third ICU medical flight, so I know the drill. I completely trust the amazing critical care air transport team to take great care of Bryce in the air.

Love, Cathy

Facebook Update: Sunday 11/25/12

This will be my last update from Hawaii. We are getting ready for take-off. Bryce is in extremely great hands right now. The Air Force Critical Care Air Transfer Team of doctors, nurses, and cardiopulmonary technicians are just incredible.

Bryce looks a little rough today. His temperature is nearly 102 degrees, and he is already on antibiotics for a urinary tract infection. Two days ago he got dehydrated because one of the machines that give him his water broke. It wasn't giving him any water at all, and unfortunately, a couple shifts passed before one of his nurses finally noticed.

Please continue to pray for Bryce. He has been through a lot in the last six weeks, and flying for many hours will take another toll on his body.

We will land in Virginia sometime on Monday. I can't wait to get Bryce started in the traumatic brain injury therapy. As much as I wish I could go back in time and protect Bryce from this horrible accident, I believe something wonderful will come from this situation, somehow, someday! God is in control, and I don't have to worry.

Love, Cathy

Life Offline

The trip from Hawaii to Richmond was in a KC-135 refueling plane. About halfway into the flight, one of the crew members took me down to see the refueling system. I had to lie down in the bottom of the plane while a crewman lay next to me and showed me the fueling boom. It was a once-in-a-lifetime experience for me.

They told me we were over Las Vegas. I looked out the window and could see all the beautiful lights on the ground. I lay there soaking in the amazing view, taking a much-needed break from our serious reality.

It was a long overnight flight, and we landed in Richmond on the 26th of November, my wedding anniversary.

As soon as we arrived in Richmond, they rushed Bryce to the ICU at the Hunter Holmes McGuire VA Medical Center and placed him on the ventilator again. Traveling is extremely hard on patients in Bryce's condition, so they slow everything down in the body, trying to keep the patient as stable as possible.

After arriving at the hospital, Bryce spent the next 24 hours in the ICU, once again being assessed by his new medical team. They moved him to 2B, the Polytrauma Unit, where he was placed in a regular hospital room—his first private room after all this time.

He was connected to various tubes, receiving oxygen through his trachea, and stuck with various IV needles. He clearly did not appear to be someone who was qualified to be an active participant. But that was okay. They were giving him a chance to emerge anyway, and I was so grateful.

Facebook Update: Monday 11/26/12

Today I met with Bryce's new doctor, Dr. Ajit Pai, who seems amazing! I also met quite a few members of the Polytrauma staff. They each left a great impression, and I can tell they truly care about Bryce's condition. I am absolutely convinced that they "get it" when it comes to traumatic brain injuries. I know Bryce is in the best place possible to recover.

This is the plan. They are giving Bryce ninety days in their "Emerging Consciousness Program," starting tomorrow, to prove he can communicate with us. It can be via blinks, hand-waving, giving a thumbs-up, or any other way he is able to let us know he understands us.

It must be a clear signal though, a repetitive one, to alleviate any doubts it is being done intentionally.

If Bryce can find a way to consistently communicate with us within the ninety days, he will automatically be enrolled into the VA's traumatic brain injury program.

If Bryce is unable to communicate with us within the ninety-day period, they will have to change course. He will have no choice but to be moved home, or to a nursing home. Note: He would be coming home. We will not move him to a nursing home!

So with all this said, please pray with me for Bryce to communicate with the staff quickly, and happily stun each and every one of them! This is not too much to ask and pray for! Miracles happen every day and I am not going to give up expecting ours!

Life Offline

Now that we were in Virginia, near family and friends, it was important that we established guidelines for visitors. I had a hard time setting and enforcing boundaries in Japan and Hawaii. But when I got to Virginia, I learned that this VA hospital was all about boundaries. They understood brain injury and how to treat it. This hospital was a controlled environment for the sake of the patients and their families.

I talked to the case managers and told them about Gwyn and some of the experiences I had with her. I explained that it wasn't her fault or my fault; it was just this awful trauma causing too much extra pain in an already painful situation.

"Do you want visitors?" the case manager inquired.

"No, except for military personnel."

"Okay, how about family?"

"No, except for Jim and Madison."

The case managers worked with us to come up with a plan. Since Jim and I already had a conversation about limiting any further visitors and he wanted to protect me from anything that might cause me extra problems, we decided to limit almost all visitors from coming to the hospital. I shared this new policy on the prayer page:

Facebook Update: Monday 11/26/12

As much as I would like to have visitors, please do not show up without having a clear invitation from me first. The next seven to ten days will be crazy as the Polytrauma team addresses Bryce's medical concerns and stabilizes him. Once settled, he will be set up on a routine with all kinds of therapies throughout the day. I would prefer to have a little time to get a feel for things before I have guests coming and going out of his room. I promise to let you know when we are comfortable with the schedule and can properly welcome visits.

Thank you so much for your continued prayers!

Love, Cathy

Life Offline

Once Bryce and I made it to Richmond, Gwyn immediately came to see us. During her second visit, she told me that her husband had agreed for her to come up to Richmond to stay with me and Bryce for a couple days and nights each week. I just needed to let her know which days would be best.

I am sure it was not what she wanted to hear, or ever expected, but I told Gwyn that I didn't want her coming back to help me. I told her I needed to go through this alone, and I needed to be brave. I could tell it hurt her feelings. She tried to change my mind, but I told her, "No, I don't want anyone with me other than Jim and Madison. I appreciate everything you have done for me, but I need to do this on my own."

Gwyn couldn't grasp what I was saying. We went around and around. She kept saying, "But Tom told me I could come." I apologized to her because she was clearly confused and hurt by me not wanting her help. She asked me if I was mad, and I told her no. I needed to do this alone, with God—and with Jim and Madison. That was the end of it.

I didn't want to tell her I was hurting and mad. This was not the time. I knew she meant well, but my heart continued to harden anyway. She looked very defeated and depressed. I meant no harm. This was about Bryce and no one else. I had to be present and go through this without any additional stress or distractions.

It was an awkward conversation, but one that I had to have.

Chapter Nine

The Ninety-Day Clock

The next day the clock started ticking to see if Bryce would emerge or be sent home for nursing care.

Facebook Update: Tuesday 11/27/12

Today, forty-five days after the accident, Bryce made it out of the ICU! Praise the Lord! He is now one hundred percent in the Richmond VA Polytrauma Unit's care.

Lots of rehabilitation will be starting soon, and I am praying and believing I will have many great reports to share over the next couple of months.

Let me tell you, the Polytrauma team doesn't play around. They are already making plans to get him up and out of that bed, and he isn't even awake yet.

As soon as they shared this with me I immediately had visions of "Weekend at Bernie's," thinking of my son being propped up all over the unit (lol). I guess God knew I needed a laugh because I sure did. They said they have ways to do it and that it will help him, so I'm in.

Seriously, I am comforted knowing they plan to do anything and everything they can think of to get Bryce to wake up and back to good health. What a blessing!

Specific prayer requests:

1. For Bryce to wake up, blink, give me a COMA HUG, or anything that would show his sweet cognitive self to us.

2. For the autonomic brain storms to stop, and not return.

Thank you all so much!

Love, Cathy

Life Offline

Even though it was just me in Richmond, the Polytrauma Team had a family meeting on November 28. It was the first time anyone explained what a severe TBI really is. I learned the function of the Polytrauma Unit and Emerging Consciousness Program—what could happen here, what to watch for, what the process is, and how much of what I have seen on TV was inaccurate.

This whole time I had been waiting for Bryce to wake up, like Sarah, and say, "Hi Mom." I expected it to be like every movie I had ever seen on the Hallmark Channel. I was told that even if he woke up, he might not know who I am, and that could be forever.

My main question was what day EXACTLY did Bryce have to wake up in order to be able to stay and do rehabilitation at this facility? I would do anything I could to help him meet this ninety-day criteria.

They explained that if Bryce emerged within that ninety-day period and advanced to the brain rehab program, he could stay in the program as long as he continued to show improvement. It could even be small incremental improvements. If, however, he emerged and then never improved any more than just emerging, he would be sent to a nursing facility or home.

They assured me that Bryce could always come back to the brain program at any time if he had a breakthrough. The 2B Polytrauma Unit said they were there for Bryce, and for us, for life.

It was so nice to spend time with Barbara Bauserman, the Traumatic Brain Injury Polytrauma Patient and Family Education Coordinator. Up to this point, I have been trying to listen, learn, and remember as many details as I could about what to expect and what to watch for. But actually being given a binder, educational paperwork, and a written plan made me feel like I had just won the lottery!

Even if just a little, I finally felt like I had a tiny bit of security back. I was so thankful for the medical professionals! I wanted to learn as much as I could about brain injuries to help Bryce get better.

Facebook Update: Wednesday 11/28/12

Lots of education today! I apologize for such a long update tonight; but I truly believe it will help you better understand what is going on inside of Bryce. It's worth the read. I learned:

1. Bryce is still in a coma.

2. Bryce is cognitively at a level two or possibly a level two plus, on the "Rancho Los Amigos Levels of Cognitive Functioning" scale, which goes from one to ten.

3. Hollywood "coma wake up scenes" are absolutely unrealistic. Waking up from a coma is a process, not a momentary event.

Here are the first four levels of the Rancho Los Amigos Cognitive Scale:

Cognitive level one (No Response): A person at this level will not respond to sounds, sights, touch or movement.

Cognitive level two (Generalized Response): A person at this level will begin to respond to sounds, sights, touch or movement; respond slowly, inconsistently, or after a delay; respond in the same way to what he hears, sees or feels. Responses may include chewing, sweating, breathing faster, moaning, moving, and/or increasing blood pressure.

Cognitive level three (Localized Response): A person at this level will be awake on and off during the day; make more movements than before; react more specifically to what he sees, hears, or feels. For example, he may turn toward a sound, withdraw from pain, and attempt to watch a person move around the room; react slowly and inconsistently; begin to recognize family and friends; follow some simple directions such as "Look at me" or "squeeze my hand"; begin to respond inconsistently to simple questions with "yes" and "no" head nods.

Cognitive level four (Confused and Agitated): A person at this level will be very confused and frightened; not understand what he feels or what is happening around him; overreact to what he sees, hears, or feels hitting, screaming, using abusive language, or thrashing about. This is because of the confusion; be restrained so he doesn't hurt himself; be highly focused on his basic needs; i.e., eating, relieving pain, going back to bed, going to the bathroom, or going home; may not understand that people are trying to help him; not pay attention or be able to concentrate for a few seconds; have difficulty following directions; recognize family and friends some of the time; with help, be able to do simple routine activities such as feeding himself, dressing or talking.

Okay, now that you have this information, when Bryce reaches cognitive level four he will no longer be in a coma.

Specific prayer requests:

1. For Bryce's brain to be miraculously healed.

2. For everyone praying for Bryce to have faith, and believe in his healing.

3. For God to get one hundred percent of the recognition and praise for healing Bryce!

Love, Cathy

Life Offline

On November 29, seven weeks after his accident, Bryce had a PEG tube placed directly into his stomach, which allowed him to receive nourishment through an elevated gravity dispenser.

I received this encouraging note on the Prayer Page:

"I have spent the last two hours reading your son's journey from start to present, shedding tears, and praying along the way. Continue talking, squeezing, and holding his hands, because he hears you. God will guide you along this journey. He is using your son to bring complete strangers together to hear His Word.

I have faith God has something very special in store for Bryce and He will heal him when it is time. Until then I will continue to say a prayer every night for your son's complete recovery. God Bless From Iowa.

Mary

I replied:

"I agree with you! I am clinging to God for help and mercy, and I am witnessing complete strangers turn toward God for strength too! I feel like He's allowing Bryce's situation to help us all grow!"

Life Offline

On November 30, Bryce was raised into a sitting position by the physical therapists as if he were sitting on the side of the bed. It was a huge milestone to see him upright, instead of lying flat. The strain of physically sitting up took a toll on his body. The color drained from his face and he started shaking. After a few moments in this position, they were able to move him into a reclining wheelchair. They were trying to get him in touch with his different senses, to purposefully stimulate him for a short amount of time. After all this activity he was returned to his bed to rest.

I was excited to see him sitting, but at the same time, it was weird to see the scene playing out. It was as if they were playing with a doll, dressing him, feeding him, and changing his diapers. I had mixed feelings about the whole thing.

Facebook Update: Friday 11/30/12

Today Bryce was placed into a special wheelchair and was able to sit for the first time in seven weeks! I don't think words can convey how awesome it was to see my precious son stroll the halls of this VA hospital! You should have seen me running for my camera. I was snapping pictures and videos like I was a crazy lady in the paparazzi! Thank you, Lord, for this little bit of almost normalcy you allowed me to witness today! I am so thankful the emerging consciousness program exists, and that they don't let a little thing like a coma stop them from helping Bryce get better!

Please keep praying for my boy!

Love, Cathy

DECEMBER

Bryce has had a miserable day. He's been vomiting off and on since his PEG tube was placed. This is a challenging problem to have when you are lying on your back almost all the time. Aspirating is rough on the body. His oxygen levels keep dropping and they have had to turn up the amount of oxygen they are giving him through his trachea.

He is also having difficulties with his intestines and colon. For the last three weeks he has not been able to keep things moving in the right direction.

Tonight his doctors ordered an x-ray of his lungs, which confirmed something abnormal going on. They also ordered x-rays of his belly area which showed severe constipation. A third x-ray was taken of his PICC line because it has been clogged all day. They were not able to see the other end of the line in the x-ray. It was supposed to be above his heart, but they need to know exactly where it is before they pump anything through the line.

For now, they have had to stop using it completely. They started adding glucose to his IV fluids and are attempting to keep him hydrated as best they can. His doctor also decided to cut off all tube feedings so his gut can rest and also so they can figure out if there is a blockage inside of him causing these problems. They don't want his intestines or colon to burst.

Another guess is that the medications they are giving him to treat his autonomic brain storms are possibly causing his gastrointestinal system to not work properly.

There is a lot going on, and Bryce needs our prayers.

Love, Cathy

Facebook Update: Sunday 12/2/12, 8:00 a.m.

Psalm 30:5b (NKJV)
"Weeping may endure for a night, but joy comes in the morning."

Thank you so much for joining me in prayer last night! Once again, our prayers have been heard, and there is a better report this morning. Thank you, Lord!

A lot of Bryce's constipation troubles headed south and cleared the area. He has had no more vomiting, and his oxygen levels stayed in the high nineties all night long. He did have one brain storm, at four o'clock in the morning.

He sure looks peaceful this morning as he sleeps, and I am so very grateful to all of you for praying for him. I hope you can all feel my hugs!

Today will be a good day!

Love, Cathy

Today has been another tough one.

Bryce started out looking so peaceful early this morning, but things quickly changed. He has been vomiting repeatedly throughout the day. He is still only getting IVs and his medications, but nothing is staying down.

He aspirated twice today, and both times it took quite a while to get his blood oxygen level back into the safe zone.

Tomorrow his medical team will try to figure this out with more tests. I know his doctor is also waiting on the results of a pneumonia test, as he has had dark yellow secretions showing up when he is suctioned for the last two days. The on-call weekend physician said that they may also run a test to see what is going on inside his stomach, intestines, and bowels, since something is clearly not working correctly.

I put a cold washcloth on his head and I am just praying he will get better. I feel so terrible watching him suffer. I can't say for sure he knows he's suffering, but I hate every second of it anyway!

I have always been the kind of Momma that tries to fix anything and everything that could possibly cause my kids pain or heartache, even when they didn't ask for it. You know the kind of Momma that at times sticks her nose too deep into situations? Yes, I admit, I have even been a tad bit too

controlling and bossy at times trying my best
to rescue them from what I thought were
unhealthy situations. Now here I am, sitting
in a hospital with my son in a coma for fifty
long days, and there is nothing I can do to
fix him.

I can't control the situation or make any of
this go away. It is a tough place to be.

With all that said, I am still able to pray,
and I can rally the troops to pray with me!
Pray that each and every cell in his body
lines up with God's perfect will for his life,
and that he be healed completely!

Thank you!

Love, Cathy

Life Offline

We received the results from the tests, and they confirmed that
Bryce had pneumonia. From the beginning, the doctors told us
patients in Bryce's condition typically die from either an infection
or pneumonia. So now I was afraid that death was imminent.

Within the first week of seeing Bryce in Japan, I made a deal with
God: "Please heal him or take him home with you, but PLEASE
DO NOT LEAVE HIM LIKE THIS!"

I never wanted to have to decide what happened to Bryce. We
wanted God to make the decision, and not us.

Bryce is having a better day. Thank you for your continued prayers. I will send out an update later if there are any changes on his condition.

One last thing that is heavy on my heart, I want to publicly thank my marvelous husband, Jim! He was unable to go to Japan when the accident happened; he is the sole provider for our family, and he has had many ongoing work obligations to fulfill. He is working day and night, doing everything in his power, so that when the time is right and this is all over, we still have an intact home for our family to come home to.

Jim has been my rock, my strong tower, the one I call when I can't take another second of the pain and heartache I feel for Bryce's situation. He is also looking after Madison, helping with the chores, taking care of our animals, the lawn, and overseeing everything else that needs to be done. I am so thankful to have a husband with a plan, and a desire to take care of and provide for his family without complaint. You are my hero, Honey!

Thank you!

Love, Cathy

Life Offline

Here is another word of encouragement from the prayer page:

"Cathy - I wanted to send you a note and tell you that I follow your posts with a Mother's heart! My daughter graduated from AF Basic Training on June 1st and has been going through the training pipeline to become a Loadmaster. I felt a connection to you as a fellow AF Mom.

I can't imagine what you went through when you got that call, and the time it took you to get to Japan. My heart went out to you as you were traveling, and my prayers went up. I watch every day for encouraging reports, and I pray for your son for a complete miraculous recovery.

Just know that there is a world of people out here, moving through your life, that you don't even know about, and we are all praying to a God who does the most amazing things! I'll keep following, and praying for a miracle.

Bonnie"

I loved knowing that I had wing sisters all over the world who were not only praying for their hero but also praying for mine!

Bryce's weekend was miserable, but he does seem to be improving. He is still moving things along in his stomach and colon, and there has been no more vomiting yesterday or today. Last night, his medical team decided to turn his tube feedings back on.

Interesting note: They explained to me that not only is Bryce in a coma, but some of his automated body functions are still slowly waking up on the inside too. The normal functions of his stomach, intestines, and bowels are not working properly yet. Add in all of the side effects of numerous medications and you can understand why he is having issues.

Michael Dardozzi, Bryce's speech therapist, came by and made different sounds using bells, music, knocks, and taps to see if he could elicit a response from Bryce.

One thing for sure, he is definitely able to hear. I was previously told that he may have lost his hearing. Then a couple days ago I dropped something off my tray in his hospital room and the second it hit the floor Bryce's eyes popped wide open, for a couple of seconds. I had clearly interrupted his coma sleep, and it was a beautiful thing.

Love, Cathy

Life Offline

The brain is still not fully understood, even by the experts. They know what certain areas are supposed to do, and they can make their best guesses. In the end, no one really knows if patients like Bryce understand deep inside themselves or not.

When brain cells die, they never come back. But if you are young enough, the brain is so smart, it can sometimes learn to reroute itself. So with Bryce, we were told age was on his side. He was still young enough that his brain could possibly learn to reroute certain areas. So this was our hope. We were also told that this doesn't happen overnight. It typically takes a long time. But at least we had some HOPE.

Facebook Update: Wednesday 12/5/12

Bryce is continuing to have his brain storms -- medically referred to as "Paroxysmal Autonomic Instability with Dystonia" (PAID). The symptoms include: fever, high blood pressure, high pulse rate, high respiratory rate, intermittent agitation, excessive sweating, and rigidity -- or "posturing," which involves his arms and legs being held straight out, his toes pointing downward, his head arching back, and his teeth clenching.

For Bryce, they have tried different medications to help stop the storms. The only relief we have seen is with the regular use of heavy opiates and these medications are not helping him wake up from his coma.

In fact, they are knocking him out so much that it is causing his blood pressure and heart rate to fall way too low at times. These medications are also making rehabilitation treatments with his therapists nearly impossible.

Here is the plan as I understand it. We have to pray Bryce's doctors can find the right medication mixture to treat this awful condition. Or better yet, pray that the condition would cease altogether.

Thank you, Prayer Warriors!

Love, Cathy

Life Offline

This Facebook post touched my heart:

"Father God, we know your will shall be done. We know you will give us grace no matter what you choose. We have been given hearts that know there is a purpose in pain, we are truly grateful for that grace, as there is much pain in this fallen world.

Please, Abba, Father, we bring Bryce Powers before your throne that you may be glorified.

Raymond"

I was invited to join a caregiver support meeting. It was nice to sit and listen to other caregivers share their thoughts, stories, challenges, and milestones. It was also helpful for me to be able to share some of my own feelings. I shared how difficult it has been for our family to cope with our new life and reality. Everything changed for us in an instant, and our family is barely hanging on.

The leader of the group shared that Bryce may be the one with the major injuries, but he was not the only one affected. She used the example of a bomb blowing up Bryce's bedroom in our house. Even though it would nearly destroy his bedroom, our entire house would also be affected. There would be smoke, debris, and damage spread throughout our home.

She explained that it's important to realize that all of us have been hurt and that we cannot expect to go through this blast without taking time to nurture our own injuries as well. This made a lot of sense to me.

We also learned about the concept of "ambiguous loss."

In the midst of this ordeal, some people would say to me, "At least Bryce didn't die in the wreck." This was true, but in reality the Bryce that we knew was gone in an instant after his accident. He was alive, but he was no longer fully alive. This is known as an "ambiguous loss."

I felt like life was already permanently ruined for Bryce, and for all of us, but I didn't know what to call it. It was so helpful to me to hear that there was an actual term for the feelings I had been secretly carrying inside me. I was not a bad mother for feeling this way. I was normal. This was my new normal.

We were dealing with loss even though Bryce's body was still breathing and his heart was pumping. We were grieving already, and it was okay. This was part of the process.

Later the doctors gave me a book called *Ambiguous Loss*, by Pauline Boss. Here's a little snippet:

"When a loved one dies we mourn our loss. We take comfort in the rituals that mark the passing, and we turn to those around us for support. But what happens when there is no closure, when a family member or a friend who may be still alive is lost to us nonetheless? How, for example, does the mother whose soldier son is missing in action, or the family of an Alzheimer's patient who is suffering from severe dementia, deal with the uncertainty surrounding this kind of loss?"

Boss explains that all too often, those confronted with such ambiguous loss fluctuate between hope and hopelessness. After extended suffering, these emotions can deaden feeling and make it impossible for people to move on with their lives.

Thankfully, the central message of this book is that people can heal and life can move on.

When Bryce suffered his brain injury, the Bryce we knew and loved was pretty much instantly gone. Yet, lying there in front of us, Bryce was still alive. So internally we were all facing a huge loss. But there was no funeral, no big ceremony marking the fact that Bryce was gone. We were left in limbo of sorts.

We had to hold on to the hope that he was still with us, but underneath, the mixed emotions of him clearly not being here anymore were staring us in the face and punching us in the gut.

Almost every day, Bryce and I participated in what I called *Weekend at Bernie's* events where the staff propped him up in a chair as though everything was normal. Had it not been me and Bryce doing these things, I would have thought this was crazy. But in this new TBI world, everyone acted like it was perfectly normal to prop up a person in a vegetative and comatose state and just live life. Again, this was the new normal.

But everything inside me was screaming, "NOT NORMAL! OH MY GOD, HELP US. NOT NORMAL."

Bryce may have received the most damage in the "bomb blast," requiring the most immediate help, but the other three injured members of our family were trying to get Bryce the help he needed so he wouldn't die. We were using all of our resources for him, but in doing so, we were barely able to help each other, or even ourselves. We were all terribly injured, and yet most people didn't recognize how deep our wounds were.

Of course, at the end of the day, because we weren't in the car wreck, most of our family and friends didn't realize we were in the HUGE BLAST. So we suffered through, ready to collapse at any moment, and we tried our best to survive. We hoped that someone would notice the red blood streaming out of us before it was too late.

As a family, we were left in a state where we couldn't really grieve the loss of our son and brother. We were suffering as if there was a loss on the inside, and perplexed that there was no way to mark or deal with this loss on the outside.

Learning about ambiguous loss really helped me to see that I was not going crazy or being negative when I felt some of these awful feelings and had some of these horrible thoughts. I had a good reason to feel like Bryce's life—and our lives—were ruined. I was grieving a very real loss that was still undefined and confusing.

Chapter Ten

Family Reunion

Facebook Update: Thursday 12/6/12

Bryce had a much better day today! Since this morning, he has only had two brain storms! This is a huge answer to our prayers, especially considering that just two weeks ago he was having them every hour! Hopefully he will continue having less and less, and soon, like tomorrow please, stop completely!

Secondly, he was able to do his therapies today because he was not over medicated.

I can't wait to see Jim and Madison in a couple more hours! I know they are both excited to see and spend time with Bryce again. They will also be getting the grand tour of the VA Hospital and Polytrauma Unit.

It seems people are praying all over the world! Thank you so much!

Love, Cathy

Life Offline

Jim and Madison made it safely to Richmond at two o'clock in the morning. We met in the hospital lobby, went straight up to Bryce's room and had ourselves a genuine Powers' family reunion! It was wonderful to be together as a family again!

Jim and Madison both noticed signs of healing and improvement in Bryce since they last saw him in Hawaii.

Later in the day, after some much-needed rest, we met with Bryce's team of doctors to receive their report on his condition. We were able to see all of Bryce's CT scans, MRIs, and x-rays in chronological order since day one. We now had a much better understanding of how he suffered such devastating injuries, even though he was wearing his seat belt.

Jim and I kept trying to make sense of it all before today. Now, with the doctor's help and the use of an actual model of a brain, we walked through how things most likely unfolded the day of Bryce's accident.

We also learned just how fragile the human brain is. We saw in black and white all of the areas inside and outside our son's skull that have been injured. Some of it was almost too much to handle. They said this is going to be a long road to recovery, a marathon of sorts, with no promise that he will ever get better.

There is so much that even experts don't fully understand about the brain. They don't know for sure what Bryce's recovery will look like.

We didn't have blinders over our eyes, thinking that all would be perfect for Bryce. We were not in denial. We simply and actively chose as a family to hold on to hope. We were trusting and believing Bryce would have a miracle healing!

We had nothing to lose and so much to gain by holding on to our faith!

Facebook Update: Saturday 12/8/12

Today we played Bryce a few of his favorite songs and YouTube comedy acts, trying to get a reaction. There was none. We did end up making a list of his favorites and I will continue to play clips for him every day. Madison wanted to play Miley Cyrus or Justin Bieber, because they are his two least favorite musicians (lol) to see if that would spark any responses – but we decided not to.

We also put together a large photo book with some of our favorite family photos. It was hard to look back at happier times without getting emotional. Someday when he is awake it will be a nice way to reacquaint him to his life.

Today marks eight full weeks since the accident. I hope and pray he will wake up soon. I know I tend to be impatient, so I need strength to calm down and keep trusting the Lord. Bryce must still need a little more healing rest. I will wait.

Thank you.

Love, Cathy

Facebook Update: Sunday 12/9/12

It sure was nice to spend a couple days with Jim and Madison. They took me shopping, bought me food for the Fisher House, bought me some new Christmas pajamas, a warm coat, and a new pair of fuzzy gloves to keep me warm when I walk to the hospital each day. They are so sweet.

As you can probably imagine, this has been a pretty tough pill for our family to swallow. If I am completely honest, some days are nearly impossible to get through. It's easy to start lashing out at each other when we are tired, afraid, or just discouraged at times along the way. I have heard stories about families completely falling apart when the stress levels rise, and everyone loses their control.

I don't want that to be the story for our family, so please say an extra prayer for us to be able to hang on to the promises of God and not fall apart at the seams. More tears were shed this weekend than probably the last month combined, but thanks to God, we made it through together.

Life Offline

There was such great tension that everyone was fighting. Jim would turn on the TV, and I would angrily order him to turn it off! I was concerned about the unnecessary noise!"

Then he'd touch some medical device and I'd say, "No, don't touch that! The doctor said, blah, blah, blah." Instead of teaching him what I had learned, I was chasing him like a toddler, smacking his hand, saying, "Stop, stop, stop."

And Jim was thinking, "I'm the man of this house. Why did I even come here?"

Then Madison was being a brat, and Jim was mad, and I was being mean.... It was the most horrible time.

Facebook Update: Tuesday 12/11/12

Today Bryce was able to sit propped up in his wheelchair for five straight hours! Not only is this good for his body, but he was also on room air. He is usually on oxygen and they took it off this morning just to see how he does. Their goal was to keep him up for about an hour and a half. He blew that goal out of the water!

I have mentioned before that Bryce is on a special medication called amantadine, which is a stimulant medication they are using to try and help him wake up. Tomorrow his doctors will raise his dosage to two hundred milligrams, given twice a day, which is the highest level they currently use.

I'm excited at what the Good Lord has in store for Bryce's future, and I believe in his eventual healing! I believe, I believe, I believe!

Love, Cathy

Facebook Update: Wednesday 12/12/12

The physical therapists put Bryce on an Erigo standing machine for five minutes. Just think about this for a minute, Bryce is in a coma, and yet he is spending time sitting and standing up. Amazing!

His physical therapists are strengthening his muscles and increasing his stamina so when he does wake up, he'll be that much closer to better health! It's very encouraging to me to see my son given every opportunity to heal here.

Last week when I shared, "I just know something wonderful is getting ready to happen!" Well I still feel that way. Every single day I am noticing little things in Bryce, like an eyebrow lifting, or hands moving toward his neck as if to grab at a tube. I believe something is happening for sure. He is going to wake up. I know it. I sure miss him.

Thank you for not giving up, for continuing to pray for his complete healing, and for all your support. I am also thankful for the beautiful and inspirational cards, notes, letters, and emails we've received!

I want you to know that because of our amazing God and divine prayer warrior support, our family has been blessed with peace. Even in the midst of this terrible storm, we have hope.

By the way, I am doing a Skype interview with WSOCTV news in Charlotte, NC, tomorrow morning. It's a blessing to have a home community that cares about wounded warriors.

Love, Cathy

Facebook Update: Thursday 12/13/12

Today was another good day. Bryce sat up in his wheelchair for a few hours, stood up with the help of his physical therapists for five minutes, and was paid a special visit by an adorable Corgi therapy dog. This cute little dog sure loved on Bryce. I lost count of the number of kisses Bryce received.

Life Offline

I went home to the Fisher House on this night, went straight up to my room, closed the door, turned off the light, and just started sobbing. I was so tired, and I was desperate for God to help Bryce! I was beyond exhausted. I couldn't even get on my knees to pray, so I just started begging God to forgive me for everything I could think of that I had done wrong in my life. I pleaded on behalf of Bryce, for his sins to be forgiven, for our family's sins to be forgiven, and even asked if He would please forgive all of our relatives for any sins we have collectively committed!

I was beyond desperate and was trying to think of anything that might convince God to have mercy on Bryce and wake him up! Still sobbing, I cried out, "Please Jesus, heal Bryce!"

Suddenly in my mind I saw Sarah, the injured passenger from Bryce's car. I saw her broken body with injuries from the crash and immediately I was overcome with a wave of shame and guilt. I knew Bryce was the one driving. It might have even been his fault she was injured so badly. We still don't know exactly what happened that day. I began wondering if that is why she woke up and Bryce didn't.

Heartbroken, I surrendered, and said to God, "Why would you heal him?" Before I could even finish my sentence, I heard out loud, in a very clear, audible male voice, "I will heal him in seventy days."

"What? God, is that YOU? You will heal him in seventy days? I heard you say it! Okay, God, I believe you will heal him in seventy days! God, if this is a test of my faith, I believe you! I know you are the Healer! Thank you, God! Thank you, Jesus!"

I flipped the light on, grabbed a calendar and started counting seventy days forward. If this voice was truly from God, Bryce would be healed on February 21.

I truly believed God would heal Bryce on February 21. I even called Jim and Madison and told both of them about the miracle we can expect to happen for Bryce. There was no doubt in my mind.

Chapter Eleven

Believing for a Miracle

This Momma is thankful for another good day with Bryce. Thanks to you, Bryce has many cards, pictures, and notes hanging up all over his hospital room. When he wakes up, he will have plenty of interesting and lovely things to look at!

The McGuire VA Medical Center had a special Christmas dinner for our hospitalized active duty military veterans and their caretakers this evening. Of course Bryce didn't get to attend, but they encouraged me to go. Santa was there and so were a bunch of his elves. We had a nice dinner, a short program, and then everyone received a big stocking full of goodies. Bryce's stocking is super big! I hope he will be able to take a sneak peek inside of it this year!

Facebook Update: Saturday 12/15/12

Today Bryce had his first shower in nine weeks. He has been kept very clean through daily sponge baths, but early this morning they put him on a gurney and wheeled him into the shower room. I hope it was a nice, refreshing feeling for Bryce.

He is still having brain storms every day, though the frequency does seem to have slowed a bit. He typically has three to four per day now.

When it happens, his muscles get so tight that he actually raises his whole body off the bed, except for his feet and his head, which are holding up the rest of him. Every time I see this, I cringe. I keep thinking that it can't be good for his injured skull to have all that pressure pushing against it. Thankfully, every time a storm erupts, Bryce receives a shot of medication that helps calm him fairly quickly.

Specific prayer requests:

1. For Bryce's brain storms to completely cease, permanently.

2. For Bryce to wake up enough so he can find a way to communicate with me and his doctors.

3. For Bryce to be pain free and infection free.

4. For Bryce to be miraculously healed by his Creator.

Thank you for praying!

Love, Cathy

Life Offline

I remember thinking at this time, "My life is ruined. I just want to give up."

So many people on Facebook would tell me things like, "You're so inspirational," and "I'm asking your Jesus to come into my heart because I want him to be my Jesus." I quickly realized that I could never be 100% real on Facebook. I was glad that our story was helping others, but I felt so weak and lonely at times. I knew we were far from perfect, and I didn't want to lie. I just didn't always tell the whole truth. I guess we are all like that, both online and in our real lives.

Facebook Update: Sunday 12/16/12

Bryce has continued to have brain storms today. It's so tough to watch him go through these physical trials, knowing there is nothing I can do outside of praying for God to make them stop. It's also frustrating to watch him spend another day in his bed. Yesterday he was also unable to get into his wheelchair because of the same brain storming issues.

I'm increasingly aware of the internal attacks trying to take over in my heart and mind. Part of me wants to march into the hospital tomorrow and demand they do something else, anything else, to make Bryce better now! That same rebellious part of me wants to start blaming the doctors and the nurses, or anyone else I can think of for that matter.

I'm frantically grasping for control in this situation, and desperately trying to find a way to help my son survive.

Only with God's help will I be able to stop my panicking and blaming. I pray, let go of the reins, and take a deep cleansing breath. God is my refuge. He is the only one strong enough to help me wade through these deep, treacherous waters.

It brings great comfort knowing God is not worried about, surprised, or even slightly overwhelmed by what's happening in Bryce's life.

Tonight, I will not worry or be anxious. I will be thankful Bryce is still alive, and determined to keep praying and placing my full trust in God. His ways are far above my ways. I'm counting on Him to work out all the details in this situation, and somehow bring about good things for Bryce in His perfect timing.

God's Word says:

Philippians 4:6-7 (NIV)
"Do not be anxious about anything, but in every situation, by prayer and petition, with thanksgiving, present your requests to God. And the peace of God, which transcends all understanding, will guard your hearts and your minds in Christ Jesus."

I am so glad this verse is in the Bible!

Please join me as I continue to pray for Bryce to be miraculously healed and fully restored by God, in His perfect timing.

Love, Cathy

Facebook Update: Monday 12/17/12

Today may have started with more brain storms, but it ended with renewed hope and faith.

When I arrived at the hospital early this morning, the first thing I saw was Bryce having another horrible storm. They gave him his shot of opiates, then his body relaxed and returned to normal. I, however, reached my Momma pain threshold. I left his hospital room in uncontrollable sobs.

I found a safe, private little space, and called my husband, Jim, hysterical and desperate for his calming and supportive words. He delivered, and I got my head twisted back on in the right direction.

A little time passed and Bryce was able to go to his therapies. They had him sitting up for hours in his wheelchair, and even got him up on the standing machine for a few minutes.

After therapy, they let me push Bryce in his wheelchair around the unit for a bit. I was able to wheel him over to a young, medically retired, Air Force Senior Airman, David Rogers. David also suffered a severe traumatic brain injury overseas, just a little more than three years ago. He had come to the Polytrauma Unit with his Mom today to visit old friends.

It didn't take me long to realize David is absolutely awe-inspiring and wonderful. He is still wheelchair bound and unable to speak words via his mouth, but he types sentences into his special computer and then pushes a button, and his words are spoken aloud via computer voice.

He is so sweet and loving, and he has the most beautiful and contagious smile you've ever seen! He told me about Jesus coming to him when he was in a coma and he asked me if he could pray for Bryce. I said, "Yes, please!"

I have a photo of David bowing his head and laying his hands on Bryce, praying for his fellow Air Force brother to be fully healed and restored!

I am so humbled, thankful, and out of tears. Every time I look at the photo of David praying for Bryce, I can't help but thank God for sending him to us!

Love, Cathy

Chapter Twelve

Christmas in a Coma

Facebook Update: Wednesday 12/19/12

Bryce had a fairly decent day. His nurses got him up, dressed, and into his wheelchair. They did their best to keep him on his regular routine in spite of the infection.

I was blessed this evening with a delicious and fun dinner out with representatives from a nonprofit organization that caters to wounded warriors. They took a group of us, both patients and caregivers, to the Botanical Gardens in Richmond for a scrumptious catered meal and then we each received a ticket to the "Gardenfest of Lights" tour. I was also given two additional tickets for Madison and Jim so we can go together as a family this weekend.

The representatives have been so kind, caring, and helpful to me. I can tell they truly love supporting the wounded troops and the families standing beside them!

Facebook Update: Thursday 12/20/12

Get ready for a Christmas miracle, because it's very evident to me that my son is trying to wake up. There have been small signs for a couple days, and today I sense even more.

For about a month now Bryce's eyes are sometimes open. I've been telling the doctors that I have felt a connection every once in a while when I have looked at Bryce. It's like our eyes lock for just a moment and I can feel a zap straight into my heart that Bryce is in there and he knows who I am.

The staff usually tells me it may be just a reflex that I am seeing, but not to give up hope. Then they follow up with another comment reminding me that the patient's family is usually the first to notice when these things do indeed start happening.

So today I sensed more connections with Bryce every couple of hours. To me, Bryce was absolutely one hundred percent looking at me when I spoke to him. If I stood on his right and spoke to him, he would open his eyes and look toward the right. Then, when I moved to his left and spoke to him, he would look toward the left.

In the medical world, this "following with your eyes" is called tracking. He wasn't fast, and he didn't do it every time, but he did do it! Today the doctors, nurses, and therapists saw it happening too!

He is slowly but surely coming back to us! Praise God! I believe in miracles. Yes I do!

Love, Cathy

Life Offline

I received this on the prayer page:

"Cathy, I pray for Bryce and your family many times throughout the day, and read your updates faithfully. I just wanted to stop by and tell you again what a strong woman you are and how much your inner strength and unconditional love inspire me to be a better mom and person.

I wish I could give you a hug and take some of your stress and worry away, but all I can do is have positive thoughts and pray. My hope and prayer is that we all have a Christmas miracle and he wakes up. Much love and respect from a Military Mom in Arkansas.

Andrea"

Facebook Update: Friday 12/21/12

Jim and Madison made it safely to Richmond. They came right up to Bryce's hospital room and wanted to see firsthand if he looked or acted any different since they were last here. They saw him tracking for a couple seconds, and both agreed his color seemed to look better. Most of the day, they saw Bryce resting with his eyes closed.

Madison made a comment about Bryce needing a haircut soon (lol). She was impressed when I told her that the VA hospital has barbers that come right to the patient's bedside to cut their hair.

The hospital also added Jim and Madison to the In-patient Dining Facility List. This means we each receive three meals a day delivered to Bryce's room. This is such a blessing because we don't have to worry about leaving the hospital in search of food or restaurants, so we get to spend even more time by Bryce's side.

We are all excited to be spending Christmas together. We are holding strong, trusting the Lord, and continuing to pray for a miraculous healing in Bryce's brain.

Facebook Update: Saturday 12/22/12

Today was all about spending quality family time together taking care of Bryce. Jim even taught us the proper way to shave him. I'm convinced he enjoyed all the extra love, pampering, and foot massages we gave him.

Bryce's white blood count continued to fall today, and his C-reactive proteins also dropped back in to the normal range. This is great news! The strong antibiotics are killing off the infections!

Life Offline

Thankfully, the day was peaceful. We all got along well and took care of Bryce, and there was no weird or extra tension. We seemed to finally be living our "new normal" about as best as a family in our situation could.

Then in the evening, everything changed. Huge amounts of tension built up. Jim seemed to be crawling with anger, and this combined with my smart mouth and Madison's rolling eyes just about brought on World War III. It was another night of eggshells and mass tension for the Powers family. We left the hospital, went to the Fisher House, and all of us went to bed not speaking to each other.

Facebook Update: Sunday 12/23/12

Today has been a rough day. Bryce has had back-to-back brain storms since early this morning. Each time they have had to give him a shot of opiates to make them stop, and after a short relief period, the storming returns for another round.

We are praying with him, talking to him, and playing some of his favorite Christmas songs.

We know our God can quiet these brain storms! We have faith that he will be fully and miraculously healed if it be God's will for his life!

Facebook Update: Monday 12/24/12

I would like to wish everyone a very Merry Christmas Eve!

Bryce has had a repeat day of brain storming, but it hasn't licked him. Nope. He is young, strong, an American Airman, fully surrounded by thousands of prayer warriors. Something good is around the corner and I will be right here to report it when it happens.

In other news, we had an incident with a furry family member. One of our dogs bit the neighbor. Jim, already over the edge stressed, decided it best to go back home this morning to take care of our 4-legged babies. We have five Chihuahuas and a cat who also thinks she's a Chihuahua (lol). They have brought us much joy over the years. So, even though Madison, Bryce, and I will miss Jim for Christmas, our pets will be ecstatic to have Dad home!

Life Offline

On Christmas Eve, our whole family was fighting. It wasn't like a normal Christmas. We weren't really looking forward to having Christmas with Bryce like that. So it was like Christmas never even happened.

Madison and I both picked out iPads a few days before, which helped me a lot with my Facebook page. Playing on them was the highlight of our holiday, and it helped the two of us focus on something other than the stress.

What I didn't know was that one of the reasons Jim was so stressed is that he had a vision, but he didn't feel that he could tell anyone. He was dealing with all of that himself, and then our neighbor, who had been pet sitting for us, got bitten by our dog.

She called and asked if our dogs had all their rabies shots. I told her absolutely, they have all had them. I told her they go to the vet every year, but she just kept going on and on about it. The bite did break the skin, but she said it was minor and did not require any medical intervention. Even so, she kept calling me, asking me if they had their shots, and telling me she needs to know the truth. I gave her the name of our vet and told her to call them for verification. It didn't seem to stop her worrying. She asked about it so many times that I was convinced she was going to sue us. It just heaped more stress onto my already overloaded heart and mind.

Jim turned on the TV when he first arrived at the hospital, and I told him to turn it off. I told him he hadn't even seen Bryce and just nagged him about keeping the TV off. I was thinking that he wasn't willing to follow the rules that the hospital staff had given me for Bryce—that we should avoid too much noise or stimuli, unless it is purposeful and would mean something to Bryce. I was just insistent that everything be done the exact same ritualistic way. The stress this caused was horrible for everyone.

Jim made the excuse that he went home because the dog bit the neighbor. But honestly, the dog biting the neighbor was just the last straw. Madison and I ended up eating Christmas dinner together at the Fisher House after Jim left.

Madison was able to spend two weeks with Bryce and me at the hospital during Christmas break, which was a wonderful treat. She walked with me every day to the hospital and just hung out in Bryce's hospital room. We did puzzles and games, met some of the patients, and caught up on each other's lives. It was a very special time for the three of us to be together. During this Christmas season, I received this encouragement on the prayer page:

"*On this Christmas Eve I lift Bryce and his family before you. Father God, touch Bryce this day. He is yours. You knew him before he was formed in his mother's womb. Heal his brain and his body. Bring him past the storms, Lord God. Bring him out of the coma.*

Father, we lift our prayers for Bryce and his family before you, believing in your miraculous healing power to knit this son and this family back to perfection.

Patricia"

I wept as I read this beautiful and tender prayer. It was just what we all needed. Our family was completely stressed beyond our limit. We were all out of our comfort zones. I think leaving the hospital and spending Christmas with our pets was much more appealing to Jim than staying here and enduring hours of arguments with me.

I don't know what I would have done without God and all of the faithful prayer warriors continuing to lift our family up to Him.

Facebook Update: Tuesday 12/25/12

Merry Christmas! Sure hope everyone had a beautiful, love-filled day spent with people you care about. If it was a tough day, you are not alone! Just remember, joy comes in the morning.

Chapter Thirteen

Into the New Year

Facebook Update: Thursday 12/27/12

Bryce's doctors are continuing to search for a cause in the increase of autonomic brain storms. An oral surgeon checked on his four impacted wisdom teeth since he had been previously scheduled to have them removed last October. The surgeon, however, could not get any reaction from Bryce when he poked and prodded the four areas. They watch for blood pressure or heart rate to shoot up, which alerts them Bryce may be experiencing pain. His doctors decided to put his wisdom teeth situation on a back burner, saving this surgery option as a last resort.

A full body bone scan is being scheduled, to see if Bryce has any fractures from the accident that were possibly missed. This could certainly be causing the increase in brain storms.

They are definitely taking great care of Bryce, and hopefully we will all find a way to help him be more comfortable soon.

God is good! He is giving me peace throughout this journey! I am thankful our Bryce is alive and continuing to rest and heal! I am also grateful I get to be by his side every day. Of course, I am at times feeling stretched beyond my comfort zone as I wait on the Lord for our miracle, but I know that it is coming!

Facebook Update: Saturday 12/29/12

Jim, Madison, and I spent the day together taking care of Bryce. He had many brain storms, some back-to-back. It was very hard to leave him for the evening. Two steps forward, one step back.

Lots of serious conversations continue to take place throughout the day and in to the night. Bryce has sixty days left of his ninety to wake up in this facility so they can work with him in their traumatic brain injury program. They are telling us he is classified as being in a vegetative state. Even though I am with him every day, I don't like the sound of this at all!

Facebook Update: Sunday 12/30/12

Jim and Madison had a tough time leaving for home today, but with work and school commitments they simply had no choice. I am grateful for the time we did have together, and also relieved they made it home safely.

God continues to bless our family in the midst of this storm. Thank you for choosing to stay and ride it out with us, praying for Bryce until the winds stop blowing and the waves stop tossing.

Facebook Update: Monday 12/31/12

Bryce has had no brain storms in the last twenty-four hours. Praise God for touching him, and allowing him a peaceful day of rest! I am so thankful for this wonderful last day of 2012. Bring on the New Year!

I was also encouraged as I read these Bible verses today:

Matthew 8:2-3 (NIV)
"A man with leprosy came and knelt before him and said, 'Lord, if you are willing, you can make me clean.' Jesus reached out his hand and touched the man. 'I am willing.' he said. 'Be clean!' Immediately he was cured of his leprosy."

So with this verse in mind, my specific prayer for Bryce this evening is:

Lord, if you are willing, please wake up Bryce, and fully restore his brain. Please reach out your hand and touch Bryce.

Happy New Year! Stay safe everyone!

Love, Cathy

JANUARY

Here it is the first day of the New Year and Bryce has been perfectly tolerating the red cap on his trachea tube! This is a little red cap that attaches to the end of his trachea breathing tube that blocks air from going in or out, so he can relearn how to breathe through his mouth and nose again. This is great news because it brings him one step closer to having the trachea breathing tube completely removed. We should all be praising God for fresh air and breathing!

I spent New Year's Eve looking at photos on my computer. I have taken a photo of the calendar, the actual date, and then at least one photo of Bryce, and sometimes more than one, every single day since I first arrived at his ICU room in Japan. I had initially wanted a chronological photo story of Bryce and his recovery so I could share it with Jim and Madison back home, and hopefully someday also with Bryce. But as time passed, I realized I need these daily photos for myself so that on days when my heart is heavy, sad, and at times afraid for Bryce, I can easily look back and see how far he has already come.

Believe me, he has come a long way. God is so good! I am once again reminded that He is in this, and He has never left Bryce broken and alone. Thank you, Lord!

Specific prayer requests:

1. For Bryce to remain in God's perfect will for his life.

2. For Bryce to recognize me, and our family COMA HUG, and understand how much we all love him.

Thank you.

Love, Cathy

P.S. Please sign "Bryce's 21st Birthday Card" online! His birthday is next Wednesday, January 9th. Since he can't have a real one, I decided to throw him a "virtual birthday party!"

Facebook Update: Wednesday 1/2/13

Today I hired an attorney to get legal guardianship of Bryce before his medical and financial power of attorney expires this month.

Today the doctors removed the breathing tube, and red cap from Bryce's trachea. This means he has been breathing one hundred percent on his own, through his nose and mouth, all afternoon. Don't you just love the sound of that? I sure do! Another step forward in his recovery!

The brain storms are still happening, but God is giving me extra peace through them. I know they will stop when God says, "Stop!", so I am just praying Bryce has extra peace right now too.

Love, Cathy

Facebook Update: Thursday 1/3/13

We received great news today! Bryce's Polytrauma team have officially raised him to a cognitive level three, which is only one level away from a cognitive level four. Remember, a level four is when he will have actually emerged from his coma-vigil.

Praise God for this amazing news! Thank you, Lord, for your continued healing touch on Bryce!

Facebook Update: Friday 1/4/13, 11:00 p.m.

We lined his wall with special photos of our family, pets, and home. We did this with hope that it will spark good memories for Bryce when he wakes up. In good faith, I have been putting his eyeglasses on him a couple hours every day so when he does wake up, he will be able to clearly see his pictures.

Specific prayer request:

For Bryce's joints, throughout his body, to loosen and return to normal. They are getting tight, twisted, swollen, and causing him pain.

Love, Cathy

Facebook Update: Saturday 1/5/13

Bryce will be having a test next week to see if a muscle relaxant medication baclofen will help with loosening his stiffened muscles.

If the trial works, then the neurosurgeon will schedule a surgery to place a hockey puck size pump of Baclofen in Bryce's abdomen.

Bryce is blessed because a lot of doctors won't do this procedure until at least one year after severe traumatic brain injury. Bryce's doctors have decided to not wait for him to be all curled up and distorted, but to act now and save his muscles from permanent damage. I'm very thankful the military has allowed us to be here at the Hunter Holmes McGuire VA Medical Center!

Life Offline

There were over 13,000 prayer warriors signed up on Bryce's Prayer and Support Facebook Page. I learned that Madison actually stopped reading the posts, and Jim never read them.

I know that I should have been giving them this information directly, but I was so exhausted I couldn't bring myself to talk with anyone about the events of the day. For some reason, I could write everything, but it was too painful to talk about it with Jim and Madison.

I was very open and honest with the medical updates on my Facebook page, but this caused difficulty for Madison and Jim. Madison felt that she wasn't getting the personal notification from her mother and had to read it just like anyone else. She didn't feel like I was connecting with her directly; she felt like just another one of the 13,000.

We would talk every couple days on the phone, but the stress was so high that none of us really looked forward to these phone calls.

I would yell at Madison for being mad at Jim. "We're gonna get divorced. Stop it. You have to behave." Then I would say to Jim, "She's just a kid. Her brother's in a coma. Be nice." It was awful.

Of course, I was trying to be on my best behavior because in my mind I needed to be good enough for God to heal Bryce, but in my heart I was angry. Jim and Madison seemed angry too. We were hardly even speaking to each other at this point.

I couldn't talk about it to anyone, but I was convinced our family unit would never be the same. I could feel my husband and marriage slipping away, and I didn't have the strength to care.

Facebook Update: Sunday 1/6/13

Today has been a peaceful Sunday. Bryce continues to rest and I continue to pray.

Specific prayer for this day:

"The Serenity Prayer"

"God, grant me the SERENITY to accept the things I cannot change, COURAGE to change the things I can, and the WISDOM to know the difference."

Love, Cathy

Chapter Fourteen

A Happy 21st Birthday

I haven't mentioned much about the brain storms lately, but they have continued to hit Bryce's body a couple times each day and night. The pain medications always help them stop, but the arching, shaking, teeth grinding, and other symptoms never seem to get easier to watch. I sure hope Bryce doesn't remember suffering through any of these brain storms when he wakes up.

I spent this morning decorating his hospital room in preparation for his twenty-first birthday on Wednesday. Even though this will be a "virtual birthday party" I still wanted his hospital room and door to have a few patriotic red, white, and blue birthday decorations!

I'm touched to see the photos and messages pouring in on Bryce's virtual birthday page on Facebook. All across the world people are baking cakes, cupcakes, and cheesecakes. Some are even passing them out to their church groups, coworkers, friends, and families.

I love how so many folks are able to take a picture showing everyone holding a cupcake up for Bryce. I've also seen many beautiful homemade birthday signs for Bryce.

Another beautiful sentiment, our local homeless shelter back home, in Monroe, North Carolina, is serving birthday cupcakes to all the people currently staying in their shelter, so they can help celebrate Bryce's twenty-first birthday too. This is just over the top wonderful to be able to see and feel so much love and support coming this way! Thank you from the bottom of this Momma's heart!

Facebook Update: Wednesday 1/9/13

Bryce's storm-free twenty-first birthday.

Tonight, I'm completely overwhelmed and in awe of the huge outpouring of love and support you have shared with us today! What a grand twenty-first birthday party we have all documented for Bryce. I look forward to the day he will be able to see and appreciate all that has been done on his behalf!

The photos coming in are so incredibly touching. It will take a few days, or weeks, to go through them all!

I truly believe he is on the verge of waking up. When I talk to him, he seems to be zoning in on me. God is certainly hearing and answering our prayers!

Thanks again for the best "virtual birthday party" ever!

Life Offline

Jim and Madison lit up twenty-one candles on top of Bryce's favorite type of cheesecake at our home in NC. They also sent this message: "Happy 21ˢᵗ birthday Bryce! We love you! Love, Dad and Madi."

The Polytrauma medical team sang "Happy Birthday" to Bryce during their morning rounds. I was able to videotape it so Bryce could watch it when he gets better. A little while later, more staff delivered twenty-one big birthday balloons. Everyone enjoyed celebrating Bryce's birthday.

A representative from a nonprofit organization set up a table of wonderful finger foods and drinks for everyone to enjoy Bryce's twenty-first birthday celebration. Our wonderful State of North Carolina sent Bryce a huge bouquet of balloons. They were absolutely gorgeous!

The amazing ICU nurses at Hachinohe City Hospital in Japan sent super-fun pictures of a birthday party they had in Japan for Bryce. I love you, Yuko and Yoshie!

.

Facebook Update: Thursday 1/10/13

Bryce is continuing to respond to me more and more. Today when I spoke to him he opened his eyes and slowly turned until he found me. His eyes actually seemed to lock on to mine for a few seconds. Each time the empty stare was replaced with a familiar look. He did this a couple of times today. I loved this so much!

I also took Bryce on a private tour of the hospital in his wheelchair. It was nice to escape for a little while and venture out.

I took him outside for a few minutes to feel the fresh air and enjoy the sunshine. I was thankful no alarms went off when we passed through the big exit doors (lol).

I talked to him about everything that's been happening over the last three months – including his amazing prayer and support team! Love you all so much!

Love, Cathy

Facebook Update: Friday 1/11/13

After three months of being in a coma, I believe Bryce is starting to respond. I was playing a music video for him, "Blessings" by Laura Story, and it seemed to me he was truly listening to it, maybe even being calmed by it. It is one of the first times I've seen him actually look engaged, possibly understanding the beautiful healing words in the song. This was so encouraging!

Love, Cathy

Life Offline

On his 21st birthday, no one from the Air Force came to the hospital to celebrate or mark the day. Bryce had earned his third stripe on Christmas Eve, and no one from the military came out to present it to him. He had already done everything to earn it before his accident, and we just had to wait until December 24, 2012, for his promotion to become official, so we were disappointed when no one arrived to mark the occasion.

Dr. Pai heard about this, and one day he brought me into his office, closed the door, and proceeded to call one of his friends at Langley Air Force Base. He told this man that our family was here supporting our son Bryce, an active duty airman, and he wanted to know where our support was from the Air Force. He told them we were here every day, unsupported, and that this wasn't right.

Well, this definitely got things rolling in the right direction. The top AMMO Chief at the Pentagon was notified, and soon we had people from the Pentagon, Misawa Air Force Base, Langley Air Force Base, Pope Air Force Base, and Shaw Air Force Base, rallying around us. It was wonderful.

Eventually, a huge group of active duty AMMO Air Force representatives came from the Pentagon, and they apologized for dropping the ball. They made good on their promises of "no one left behind," and from that day forward, they took good care of Bryce and our family.

They said they were inspired by my Facebook posts, and they brought me a Willow Tree Angel and an AMMO coin, which was a tremendous honor.

Facebook Update: Saturday 1/12/13

Please let me take a moment to catch everyone up on Bryce's medical status. Bryce is at the bottom of the scale, a level three on the Rancho Los Amigos Scale.

With that said, I want you to know that I have witnessed a huge change in Bryce since his birthday. He's making noises and what seems to me like attempts to verbalize when I sing to him, talk to him, and play music for him.

These possible responses are new in the last few days and give me great hope and comfort!

Bottom line, I truly believe our prayers are being heard and answered! Praise God!

Love, Cathy

Chapter Fifteen

The Halfway Point

Facebook Update: Sunday 1/13/13

Today is day forty-five, the half-way point, of the ninety-day emerging consciousness program. I am praying and believing he will make it to a level four before the ninety days runs out.

Bryce had a crummy weekend filled with intestinal issues and brain storming. The rest of his time was spent knocked out from the pain and nausea medications. So, with that, of course there were no new connections made for me to share. I am, however, very thankful he was able to get some much needed rest.

Facebook Update: Monday 1/14/13

Today was a much better day for Bryce. I am so thankful for all who have been praying for him. It's such an encouragement to me. I'm positive your prayers have helped change his circumstances.

Today he had no brain storms, no intestinal or bowel troubles, and no nausea. Watching Bryce have a mellow and peaceful day is over-the-top great news for this Momma.

I have been very tired lately and I miss Jim and Madison something fierce. Only three more days and they will be here for a long four-day weekend! Thank you, Lord, for working this out.

Facebook Update: Tuesday 1/15/13

God is in control! He loves Bryce, and I place all my trust in Him completely!

Fun Facts about Bryce:

Favorite Color: *Red*

Favorite Number: *Thirteen*

Favorite Music: *Techno, classic rock.*

Favorite Movies: *Star Wars Collection.*

Favorite Hobbies: *Playing his guitar, building models, anything computer-related, anime, and X-Box games.*

Favorite Desserts: *Cheesecake, banana pudding.*

Favorite Foods: *Sushi, pizza.*

Favorite Drinks: *Black coffee, aloe vera juice.*

Favorite Verse: *Isaiah 40:31 (KJV) "But they that wait upon the Lord shall renew their strength, they shall mount up with wings of eagles; they shall run, and not be weary; and they shall walk, and not faint."*

Thank you for praying with me!

Love, Cathy

Life Offline

I saw this note on the prayer page, written by an airman from our hometown:

"Can't believe I didn't hear about this sooner, but I guess that's what being deployed will do to you. I didn't know Bryce, but it pains me to know that a fellow Airman and someone from not only my hometown, but my school is injured in such a way.

I'm proud to say that when you guys flew into Okinawa it was my unit that handled and fixed the plane so you could continue on your way. I'm praying every day for you to have a quick and full recovery. Get well soon, brother.

Jonathan"

I wrote back to Jonathan:

"First, I want to say 'Thank you for your service,' Jonathan! Second, I love and appreciate everyone in your unit in Okinawa for helping to fix our airplane --especially since we had special cargo and had to fly a long way over the ocean to get to Hawaii!

Thank you very much for taking the time to write on the prayer page, care about, and pray for your brother in arms! I appreciate you!"

Today was a great day! Bryce and I had two wonderful United States Air Force visitors from Langley Air Force Base. They presented Bryce with a beautifully framed congratulations certificate promoting Bryce to Senior Airman Powers.

They also presented Bryce with a cool Langley AFB Medics challenge coin.

I am overjoyed with Momma pride! Thank you USAF!

Love, Cathy

Facebook Update: Friday 1/18/13

For the first time since the accident, Bryce has made it a little over three days, eighty hours, without a single brain storm! I am praising God for His healing touch!

We had a family meeting with the medical team today. We have forty days left for Bryce to emerge from his semi-conscious state. He is currently teetering on the cognitive level two and level three fence.

Last week he had been upgraded to a level three, but he has not been able to stay consistent with that level. So now on paper his level has been downgraded to a level two+.

We are not discouraged. We still have our hope, faith, and our complete trust remains in God to work all things together for good!

I am beyond encouraged to have Jim and Madison here for a few days! We have spent the day loving on Bryce and attending his therapies with him. We are getting ready to go to the emerging consciousness program halfway point family meeting. After that we have an appointment with the Polytrauma neuropsychologist to make sure we are all dealing with this situation as best we can, as a family unit and as individuals.

Last, but not least, tonight Jim took me and Madison out for relaxing pedicures and massages, and then for a nice dinner. My "manly man" enjoyed the same treatment. Yes, Jim is not ashamed to admit he enjoyed the pampering as much as us gals. Today was wonderful and much needed.

Facebook Update: Saturday 1/19/13

Today was a nice, relaxing family day. We hung out at the hospital, spending precious time with Bryce.

First, we watched Star Wars, since it is his favorite movie. Then, Madison read a few chapters of *The Hobbit* to Bryce. The rest of the day was spent talking to him and playing favorite songs and music videos, the ones Bryce used to love watching and listening to before his injury.

Our primary goal was to interact with Bryce in familiar and fun ways, to help him emerge from his semiconscious state. He did not wake up today, but we feel like he knew we were there. He also made it through the day fairly peacefully, without any brain storms. Tonight makes 104 hours without a single brain storm.

We are thanking God for a great day together!

Love, Cathy

Facebook Update: Sunday 1/20/13

Tonight I am thanking God for healing Bryce of the brain storms. He has not had one since January 15. Thank you, Father God, for literally calming the storms!

Love, Cathy

Life Offline

Although I was posting optimistic news on Facebook, personally I was praying around the clock asking God to help me to overcome oppressive feelings of fear and dread. I felt so alone. I had to constantly fight the sadness, worry, and fear, trying to somehow stay positive.

This was so much bigger and scarier than anything I had ever faced. Bryce needed a miracle. I was screaming on the inside because I didn't know how to fix this. Bryce was broken. I was broken. Jim was broken. Madison was broken. Our entire family needed help, support, and answers.

Only God helped us survive this dark time. I was feeling so desperate for hope in this situation. I knew God's Word promised that He had not given me a spirit of fear, and yet I felt real and serious fear. I knew I had to be brave. I had to keep walking forward, step by step, to help Bryce come back to us someday. Every day I was praying for strength, wisdom, and mercy.

Facebook Update: Tuesday 1/22/13

I long for the day Bryce will wake up and come back to us, and back to full consciousness. I hope no one minds me sharing this part of the journey too.

Plain and simple, I miss my son and I can hardly stand it!

The last couple of days have been extremely difficult. I feel like I am fighting a huge battle both as a Momma and as a woman of faith. The war is physical, spiritual, and emotional – and it is fierce! I have been having trouble controlling the tears.

As a Momma, I can hardly stand the pain and heartache our family has felt since this tragedy began.

Specifically for me, I'm battling overwhelming feelings of fear, sadness, worry, and loss. I'm wondering how long Bryce will be frozen in this uncontrollable and devastating situation. I can only watch from the sidelines as he lays injured and broken.

As a woman of faith, I love God, trust Him, and I try my best to stand by the promises in His Word!

James 5:15 (KJV)
"And the prayer of faith shall save the sick, and the Lord shall raise him up; and if he have committed sins, they shall be forgiven him."

II Timothy 1:7 (KJV)
"For God hath not given us the spirit of fear; but of power, and of love, and of a sound mind."

Jeremiah 30:17 (KJV)
"For I will restore health unto thee, and I will heal thee of thy wounds, saith the LORD."

Please pray for me to be the kind of Momma that keeps my eyes on the Lord, fully trusting Him with every step, regardless of the emotions and fears that pop up and try to take me down!

Love, Cathy

Chapter Sixteen

It's All Right to Be Human

Facebook Update: Wednesday 1/23/13

I am so glad I was able to share how weak and wounded I have been feeling the last couple of days. Thank you for responding with amazing words of encouragement, wise suggestions, and powerful, heartfelt prayers that pointed me back in the right direction. I feel blessed beyond measure to have such loving and faithful friends who are willing to walk this journey, through good times and bad, right alongside me.

I realized this morning that I must take a time out. I needed to get away from the hospital for the day and simply refuel. I began by sleeping in. After waking, I spent time in prayer, and then read a devotional. When I finally got up, I enjoyed coffee and breakfast in the Fisher House dining room.

I checked in on Bryce and he was doing fine, so I left his room and decided to go to a caregiver support meeting instead.

I had a late lunch and then went to visit David Rogers and his family. They are functioning with their "new normal," and I would say they are thriving quite well three years after their son's devastating accident.

Witnessing this little peek into their lives gave me new hope and lots of great ideas for the future. It was exactly what I needed. I am thankful for this day of rest.

Life Offline

I received this encouragement on the prayer page:

"I want to share with you how much of an inspiration you have been to me. I am reminded daily, through you, what a powerful God we have. I start my daily prayers for your beautiful son, you, your husband, and beautiful daughter.

Until I started following you, my prayers were hit and miss and I sometimes wondered,' but I wonder no more.

You hang in there and you stay by your son. God is working! Thank you so much for sharing and for letting me be a part of your amazing miracle.

Kim"

This note encouraged me and gave me a fresh perspective. I was reminded that no matter what our circumstance, we can always trust our Mighty God to bring about something good.

Facebook Update: Thursday 1/24/13

Bryce had a tonic-clonic seizure today. Fortunately, his doctor was just a few feet away from him, as was I, when it occurred, so he was able to witness exactly what happened.

Tomorrow morning the doctors will make their decision as to how they will move forward to treat or not to treat with seizure medications. The challenge we face is that usually once you have a witnessed seizure following a severe traumatic brain injury, they treat the patient with seizure medications typically for one to three years. If not, there is a risk of another, possibly worse, more dangerous seizure happening, which could cause even more brain damage to the patient.

However, one of the biggest side effects of the seizure medication for someone in Bryce's circumstances is that it may hinder him from coming out of his vegetative state. So they do not want him to have any more of these tonic-clonic seizures, but they do want him to wake up someday. His doctors have a very tough decision to make.

Thank you for joining with us in prayer.

Love, Cathy

Facebook Update: Friday 1/25/13, 8:00 P.M.

Bryce had a good day today. He has made it ten full days without a single brain storm. I am so thankful to all of you that have prayed with me, specifically asking God to remove these brain storms from Bryce. God has answered us!

Today the doctors made the decision to not treat yesterday's tonic-clonic seizure with medication. If he has another one, they will have to treat it. So we will all have to specifically pray the seizures away too!

All is well with my soul! I am full to the brim with peace and thanksgiving in my heart. Thank you for willingly strapping into this mega roller coaster every day with me! Who's got their hands up?

Love, Cathy

Facebook Update: Sunday 1/27/13

Did you know semiconscious patients can make noise? I sure never thought about it until Bryce started making noises a couple weeks ago. He started groaning and moaning every once in a while, especially during his tough, painful workout sessions and therapies.

Today I noticed a change in his noise making. What used to be groans and moans has now changed to a sweet babbling. It reminds me of a baby that is self-soothing by making different sounds, at different volumes, while listening to its own voice. No real words are coming out, but it is definitely a beautiful babbling to this Momma's ears.

Thank you!

Love, Cathy

Life Offline

We were still waiting to find out if Bryce's accident would be determined "in the line of duty," and waiting for a decision was taking a toll on me. I tried not to worry, but everything relating to Bryce and his care was so serious and critical that it was nearly impossible to push the long list of "what ifs" from my mind.

I knew it was affecting my relationship with Jim in a negative way. If I was perfectly honest with myself, I would admit this constant stress and pressure was probably affecting every relationship I had. This worry was robbing me of peace, sleep, and joy. I hoped we wouldn't have to wait much longer for an answer.

Facebook Update: Monday 1/28/13

I took Bryce out of the hospital again this afternoon. I believe the cool, fresh air is doing him good. I love pushing him around in his wheelchair, telling him, and retelling him why he is here, what happened, and how much we love him.

Funny how after all these years with my big mouth that now God is putting my many words to good use! That is a miracle in itself! I love it!

Life Offline

Bryce had now been officially reassigned to Langley Air Force Base in Hampton, Virginia. The base sent over a group of airmen to visit. They sure made us feel cared for and loved. They brought all kinds of cool AMMO decorations to hang in his hospital room, along with a marvelous collection of AMMO challenge coins. It was so great to see them!

After they left, I was walking around the hospital smiling big, feeling very proud, and bragging to anyone who would listen to me. "Our Air Force family was here to see us today." I just couldn't help myself. I am certain it was great for Bryce's spirit too.

Facebook Update: Wednesday 1/30/13

Bryce has not had a brain storm in the last fifteen days. I would call that a healing for sure.

I love having specific prayer requests to share with everyone because when the specific prayer is answered, even though not always quickly, it is so very clear to see how God has heard our prayers and answered us. It builds my faith. Hopefully it builds your faith too. God is so good to us!

Specific prayer requests:

1. For Bryce to find a way to purposefully and repeatedly communicate with his medical team.

2. For Bryce to not have any fear when he wakes.

3. For Bryce to be miraculously healed by the Creator Himself, and to have a second chance to live a healthy, long, fruitful life, as a walking, talking testimony of God's healing grace and mercy.

Love, Cathy

Facebook Update: Thursday 1/31/13

Today was not a "good news" day. I don't want to pass on negative reports, but I also want to be completely honest as you pray with us during this journey of ups and downs. With that said, I will simply pass on today's report, then continue holding on to my hope, fully trusting God.

Today was Bryce's weekly team meeting. They have determined Bryce to be at a level two cognitively. Bryce remains in a vegetative state. His injuries are severe, and there are four separate levels of devastating injury to Bryce's brain.

The first level of injury: Bryce suffered a severe injury on the left side of his brain. He was wearing his seat belt, but there were no airbags. His head hit and broke the passenger seat, with impact on the upper left, front side of his skull, above his ear. The blunt force trauma shattered and separated the bone in that area, and also fractured his skull in many other places.

Note: Unconsciousness tends to last longer for people with injuries on the left side of the brain.

The second level of injury: Bryce suffered a severe diffuse axonal injury, similar to shaken baby syndrome. This is one of the most devastating types of traumatic brain injury. There is widespread damage to his axons and extensive lesions in his white matter tracts, causing him to remain in a vegetative state.

Note: Over ninety percent of patients with severe DAI never regain consciousness. Those who do wake up often remain significantly impaired.

The third level of injury: Bryce suffered an anoxic injury, due to a reduced amount of oxygen at some point after the accident. When oxygen levels are significantly low for four minutes or longer, brain cells begin to die. After five minutes, permanent anoxic brain injury can occur.

The fourth level of injury: A couple weeks after the accident Bryce developed normal pressure hydrocephalus (NPH), which caused ventricles inside his brain to swell and build up pressure. His brain swelled so much that it caused the curvy portions on the outside to flatten out inside his skull.

With the information from this report and all that has been documented in the last sixty-three days by the team, they have decided to go ahead and move forward with discharge plans for Bryce. They do not believe he will be waking up here at the facility, at least not now.

Our family is not going to give up our hope for a miracle. We will press on to love, take care of, and work diligently with Bryce – and do everything we can think of to wake him up someday.

In the meantime, we must follow the orders and map out a plan to get him safely home.

Please do not be devastated by today's post. I am telling you, God is good and He is not at all surprised by this medical report. He has a plan for Bryce, for us, and for you too! There are thousands of us here on this Facebook page, and most are willing to pray for a miracle for Bryce. So let's continue to do just that! I was thinking, the poorer the report, the bigger the miracle!

Thank you for not giving up!

Love, Cathy

Chapter Seventeen

The Full Ninety Days

FEBRUARY

Facebook Update: Friday 2/1/13

Here is a closer look at what discharge plans will look like for Bryce.

He will definitely get his full ninety days here in the VA Polytrauma Unit. With the type of injuries and medical needs Bryce has, they must start the planning early. The team is not tossing him out of the program prematurely, or giving up on him. They simply have the tough job of making projections of Bryce's medical condition at the end of the month and also at the end of his ninety days.

Getting Bryce home is another issue in itself. Our house is an older, modular home, built in 1995. It is the same size as a double wide trailer. After a few meetings, we have learned that we will not be able to make the required VA guideline modifications to our home as it is.

Because of this, we are faced with a decision of having to either build a new house on our property; move to another house capable of the VA required modifications; or move to a house that has already been built to the standards.

This is the only way the VA will allow us to bring Bryce home so we can continue to care for him ourselves, as opposed to placing him in a nursing facility.

We are looking at all of our options. Jim is getting his GI Bill paperwork together to see if we qualify for financing to build a new home on our land.

We also need to purchase a handicap-accessible van to help me transport Bryce to and from his medical appointments. The VA will hopefully help us with this purchase.

In the meantime, our social worker is trying to find a subacute nursing facility with rehabilitation therapies that Bryce and I can go to until the house can be built and medically equipped.

I am officially being trained on how to care for Bryce, and how to properly use the equipment he requires. I have been unofficially assisting the nurses with his care for months already, so I am confident I will be able to do a good job.

Specific prayer requests:

1. For God to provide us with financial and physical help to build a safe, adequate home, so Bryce and I can get home to our family soon.

2. For God to help us get a handicap-accessible van.

Love, Cathy

Facebook Update: Saturday 2/2/13

Bryce suffered a huge brain storm this afternoon. It just appeared out of nowhere and surprised us all. One minute he was fine, and the next he seemed to be out of breath, gasping for air, and responding as if he were in terrible pain. His blood pressure and heartbeat both shot up. Within seconds, his clothes were soaking wet from the big drops of sweat that were rolling off of his body.

I was horrified watching him suffer these terrible symptoms, unable to do anything but call out for the nurse. The nurse introduced a strong pain medication through his PICC line and Bryce's body began to relax. I know it takes a toll on his system when this happens. He has been sound asleep ever since.

I laid my hands on Bryce today and prayed for him. I have done this many times, but today, a fresh dose of peace and hope just washed right over me. I just started smiling and thanking God for having everything under control, in spite of what I see, feel, or think I know. I'm telling you, something amazing is going to spring forth out of this seemingly terrible situation.

Thank you for sharing the journey with me!

Love, Cathy

Life Offline

I'm pretty sure I would have been devastated about the reports on Bryce's multiple levels of brain injuries had I not heard that voice on December 13 say, "I will heal him in seventy days." I saw this as a test of my faith, and I really wanted to pass the test. I prayed, "Please Jesus, heal Bryce completely. I believe You will."

Facebook Update: Sunday 2/3/13

I am sensing a change in Bryce. I can't quite explain it to you, but I am telling you as his Momma, I believe something wonderful is happening within Bryce!

When I talked with Bryce today, I reminded him how much God loves him. I also told him how much we love him and that I believe God is going to heal him. It was then that I noticed a big tear running down the outside corner of his left eye. I thought it was strange, and I wiped it away.

I continued talking to Bryce about Madison, his Dad, the Air force, and Japan. Once again, he started dropping tears, one after another. I just kept wiping them away, hugging him, and telling him how much we all love him.

I have no idea if tears falling for no apparent reason are a normal thing that happens to someone in his condition, so I will ask his doctors tomorrow. As his Momma, I sense a change in Bryce and believe healing is happening.

Thank you!

Love, Cathy

Facebook Update: Monday 2/4/13, 12:00 p.m.

Please say a special extra prayer right now for Bryce. Something does not seem quite right.

He is lethargic, drooling, placid, pale, and as his Momma, I sense something is very wrong.

On Saturday, Bryce had that big brain storm that wiped him out, then he slept all day yesterday, and now today he seems to be even worse.

His doctors are going to check his blood to see if anything is off and check his urine for a possible infection. They also just took a chest x-ray because he has had a cough too.

Specific prayer request:

1. For Bryce to be comforted, and not be afraid, or in any pain.

2. For God to give his medical team great wisdom, especially in treating and caring for Bryce.

3. For God to heal Bryce completely.

Thank you! I will keep you posted.

Love, Cathy

Facebook Update: Monday 2/4/13, 6:00 p.m.

Thank you for all the extra special prayers prayed on Bryce's behalf today. He was just pitiful, and I knew I could count on you to help me lift him up to the Father for immediate relief! Just in the last hour, Bryce is starting to look much better.

The chest x-ray came back normal. The urine labs came back normal. The blood work is still being processed, so we won't know if anything is off kilter or abnormal until tomorrow.

A few days ago, his creatine and magnesium levels were a little off, so his doctors had to tweak his IV fluids and also give him a little extra magnesium. Today they are thinking that with the severe brain storm he had this weekend, which caused excessive fluid loss, his lethargy and other symptoms might be caused by an electrolyte issue. He could also be simply experiencing extreme exhaustion as a reaction to the severe brain storm he suffered. Just in case, his medical team is closely monitoring his fluids while waiting for his labs to come back and hoping he doesn't have any more brain storms in the meantime.

Tomorrow morning they are still planning to send Bryce for the baclofen trial. I believe it is scheduled for 8:00 a.m.

Specific prayer requests:

1. For every cell in Bryce's body to function properly again.

2. For Bryce to have protection from infection.

3. For Bryce's electrolyte levels to stay within the normal ranges.

4. For the baclofen trial and spinal tap to go smoothly, for the medication to bring immediate relief to Bryce's spasticity and pain issues, and for Bryce to be a good candidate for the internal pump.

Thank you for praying with me!

Love, Cathy

A long day of spinal taps.

This morning, Bryce went in for his baclofen trial. The first spinal tap was done at the L3-L4 level. They were able to tap in, but they could not get any fluid out. The second spinal tap was up a little higher at the L2-L3 level. This tap worked out nicely. They were able to inject one hundred micrograms of baclofen into his spinal canal during the procedure.

They were also able to test his cerebrospinal fluid pressure, which had been off-the-charts low. It is now in the normal range. This is great news. The shunt placed inside Bryce's brain is doing its job.

Unfortunately, after all the preparation Bryce had to endure, I was just informed the baclofen had no beneficial effect on Bryce's body. His medical team was very hopeful he would be a good candidate for the pump. Nonetheless, his spasticity issues stayed the same all day long.

I am thankful anyway.

I was pretty disappointed a couple hours ago. I called home crying, out of hope, and completely drained of strength. Jim listened to me, and then helped pick me back up with a little love, encouragement, and wise counsel. By the time I hung up the phone, my attitude had been adjusted. At this point, I am thankful Bryce's medical team took the time to try and help Bryce with his spasticity and pain issues. I also realize it is a blessing to know the baclofen pump would not have been a good option for Bryce before the device was actually surgically implanted into his body. It would have been so much worse if they did the surgery first, only to learn later the pump won't help him.

They kept Bryce lying flat all day so he wouldn't get a spinal headache. The nurse is checking his vital signs every fifteen minutes, and he is resting peacefully this evening.

Specific prayer request:

For God's perfect plan for Bryce's life to unfold before our eyes. We know Bryce was fearfully and wonderfully made by God. We will continue to praise Him. God loves Bryce and knows best how to care for His beautiful children.

Thank you for your continued prayers for Bryce.

Love, Cathy

Facebook Update: Wednesday 2/6/13

Nothing short of a miracle! God has once again heard our prayers and intervened on Bryce's behalf!

Bryce's doctors ran a test to see if he could receive the baclofen pump to help with his muscle contractions. After an initial disappointing test, they decided to try again. This time, when they began moving his arms and legs they immediately noticed a huge change with Bryce's tone and spasticity. He was so much more relaxed and limber.

The medication, which should have peaked between two to four hours after the bolus injection, was finally working perfectly. It was such a surprise! His doctor said he has never seen this happen before, and he's been doing the pump trials since 2007!

It's official! Bryce is a great candidate for the baclofen pump! I am so grateful he will soon have relief from some of his hypertonicity issues!

Our God is so amazing!

Thank you so much for praying! You are so loved and appreciated!

Love, Cathy

Life Offline

I saw this on the prayer page and it brought a smile to my face.

"Mrs. Powers,

I think you need to show Bryce this page when he gains full consciousness again. He should know that thousands of people have been waiting for him to wake up and see all the kind things that have been written on this page."

Mike

Facebook Update: Thursday 2/7/13

Today was the weekly meeting for Bryce's medical team, and he remains a level two on the cognitive scale.

This morning I decorated Bryce's room for Valentine's Day. There are red hearts plastered everywhere! I wrote the name of each patient in our unit on a heart doily, and then hung them up. I had one hundred twenty of these, so I was able to also include a personalized heart for every member of the staff. I sure hope Bryce feels the love!

Jim and Madison will be here in a couple hours. It will be wonderful to hug them both! I know it will be great for Bryce to have all of us here for the weekend!

God is so good! I trust Him completely!

Love, Cathy

Facebook Update: Friday 2/8/13

Jim and Madison made it safely to Richmond last night. Jim and I had a family discharge meeting with the medical team this afternoon. It ended up taking nearly three hours to discuss all options and details of what is to be expected in the next five or six weeks. We have a lot to think about this weekend!

The ninety days are quickly coming to an end. On Monday morning we will be giving the hospital staff our recommendation for where we would like Bryce to go next.

Our only option, outside of moving, is to build a new home from the ground up. This will take some time, at least a few months, so part of today's discussion was trying to figure out where Bryce will go next.

Specific prayer requests:

1. For our family to have clear direction, and favor, in deciding what is the best course of action to take.

2. For Bryce to be miraculously healed, fully restored, and given a second chance to live life to its fullest.

Love, Cathy

Life Offline

Back in January, our social worker introduced us to a nonprofit organization to try to help us get the ball rolling. Multiple forms were filled out in hopes that our family could attain grants for special adaptive housing, a wheelchair-accessible vehicle, and possibly some of the equipment Bryce would require at home. The representative was very kind and even offered to fill out all of our forms and file them for us. We were told there were plenty of grants that Bryce could probably qualify for, due to the severity of his injuries.

Then, in February, we received the news that Bryce was denied services and grants across the board through this organization because his military "line of duty" determination had not yet been completed. It was a confusing and frustrating time for us. We could see a little light at the end of the tunnel and desperately needed help for Bryce but were unable to reach it.

Facebook Update: Saturday 2/9/13

We have so much on our minds this evening. We're not sure how to move forward to help Bryce get the best care possible as an active duty Air Force member without stepping on some toes.

We called our congressman to discuss some of our options, but honestly the entire situation is so incredibly complicated, it has rocked us to the core.

We have been told there are no military facilities that will be able to offer quality treatment for our active duty injured son. Our choices are to let them send Bryce to a VA nursing home, if they can find one with room, or to a civilian facility.

The long-term, severe traumatic brain injury medical rehabilitation system for our military seems to be broken. Since Bryce has not yet emerged here in the time allowed, he will simply have to move along.

I want to bring him home, but I have already shared that we will have to build a new house in order to accommodate his many medical needs. Believe me, we are desperate to get him home, and we are doing everything we can think of to make that happen.

It's shocking to think our son joined the military, and after a catastrophic accident there is no military facility to look after him and help him with the therapies he needs to possibly get better. He is getting better too! Taking little baby steps maybe, but baby steps in the right direction!

Please pray for Bryce and for us, for God to help us sound an alarm to get Bryce the medical help he deserves.

Please don't think I am bashing the military either, as that is the furthest thing from my mind. I am extremely appreciative of our military. I love our brave troops. I am a proud wife of an Air Force Veteran and a proud Momma of an active duty service member. I just think something is wrong with this situation, and I want it fixed – for Bryce, and every other brain injured troop. This could happen to your son, daughter, sibling, or spouse someday.

Please do not send me messages telling me I just need to learn to "trust God more" or to "let go and let God." I do love God, and I trust Him. I am not mad at God or blaming Him for any of this. I am also not questioning my faith. I am simply just a Momma loving my son and trying my best to make sure Bryce is given every benefit he deserves to get better and be taken care of.

It was his life dream to serve his country. He made the choice as a young boy, and he realized his dream!

I hope that my being extremely transparent tonight does not come across as a person without faith or hope. I just need help for our young son. I am begging you to pray with me for a miracle solution to these huge mountains before us.

Thank you for letting me vent tonight!

Love, Cathy

Facebook Update: Sunday 2/10/13

Bryce had another brain storm today. It took two shots of strong opiates before it ceased. Thankfully, the medication knocked him out and the remainder of his day was restful.

Jim and Madison made it safely back home. It was a blessing to spend the weekend together as a family.

Bryce will be going to the operating room for oral surgery on Thursday morning. He will be having all four of his impacted wisdom teeth taken out. We aren't sure if they are a source of his brain storming. His doctors believe it is better to have them removed here where they can monitor him closely.

Thank you, Prayer Warriors!

Love, Cathy

Facebook Update: Monday 2/11/13

I shared yesterday that he had a brain storm in the afternoon. As of this evening he has now had seven brain storms in the last thirty hours. He has also been vomiting and appears to be in pain.

His doctors are trying to figure out what is causing these brain storms to start up again, especially since they had all but stopped for nearly three weeks. His lead doctor said, "This is not normal."

The bottom line is that Bryce looks miserable and needs all of our prayers. Please stop for a moment and pray.

Thank you!

Love, Cathy

Today Bryce started his day with a white blood count that had more than doubled since yesterday. He looked miserable, was extremely agitated, and was right on the verge of having a storm. His nurse and I were trying everything we could think of to keep him from brain storming full throttle. We put cool cloths on his head, rubbed his feet, and put a cool fan on him. We kept at it, but it wasn't working.

At nine o'clock this morning, a group of thirteen of our U.S. Air Force AMMO family came to visit. There were two AMMO Chiefs, one Senior Master Sergeant, five Master Sergeants, four Tech Sergeants, and one awesome wife of an AMMO Chief. They all came to the hospital specifically to visit SrA Bryce Powers and his Momma. They traveled from Air Force HQ at the Pentagon and from Langley Air Force Base.

Before they came in to his room, Dr. Pai met them in the hallway outside his door and requested that they not stimulate Bryce because of his condition. He did not want Bryce to have another day of brain storms. He also requested that no more than two or three go in to Bryce's hospital room at one time. They agreed.

I asked Dr. Pai if they could all very quietly enter Bryce's room for just a minute so I could at least snap a quick picture of them around Bryce's bed. The doctor agreed.

So they all filed in and gathered around his bed, and we snapped a couple photos. I noticed Bryce had calmed right down and no longer looked like he was going to have a brain storm, so I didn't ask any of them to leave the room.

The chiefs and I started talking very softly, while everyone else stayed pretty much silent. I kid you not, within seconds it was as if Bryce knew who they were and that they were there for him! He just relaxed and stayed calm, his eyes open, and started scanning the room from side to side. He never made a sound the whole time they were there, (about three hours), and kept his eyes open the whole time. It was just an amazing, amazing morning! I am so thankful for our Air Force family!

During their visit, they presented Bryce with an awesome AMMO flag from Misawa, Japan. It was signed by all of his AMMO family there. There was also a letter attached that said:

"SrA Bryce Powers,

We send this letter and certificate in honor of your service to our Country and the AMMO Community. We also congratulate.you on your recent promotion to Senior Airman.

The United States Air Force, and especially AMMO Community, is very proud of your contributions supporting the AMMO mission while serving overseas securing the freedoms of other countries and nations while also ensuring the security and freedoms of those back home.

We wish you a speedy recovery.

Richard W. Pennington, CMSgt. (ret)
AMMO Chiefs Association President"

They brought Bryce a beautiful Willow Tree Angel of Comfort to keep in his room, and they gave me a *Jesus Calling,* daily devotional calendar. Bryce and I were also each presented with an AMMO challenge coin!

About an hour into the visit, two more Air Force people walked in to his room. The first was AMMO Chief Van Ray (ret), and the second was Lieutenant Colonel Craig Sanders (ret). They drove up from Greenville, North Carolina, to see Bryce. During their visit, Chief Ray took his beautiful AMMO ring off his finger and placed it on Bryce's finger. He gave it to him to keep! He said a few words, told him his AMMO family cared about him, and also mentioned that his AMMO ring had been all around the world a few times. It was just so touching and made this Momma so proud!

We all gathered around Bryce's bed for prayer before they left. I cannot share in words what today's visit meant to me. Not only was it great for us to be surrounded by such brave and exceptional men and women in uniform, but I truly believe God sent them to us! He used them to calm the brain storms in Bryce. We all witnessed Bryce instantly settle when they walked into his room, and he stayed calm the rest of the day.

His latest laboratory tests came back, and even his white blood count miraculously dropped back in to the normal range. God was in this visit!

Love, Cathy

Chapter Eighteen

God's Healing—In His Time

Facebook Update: Wednesday 2/13/13

Today is exactly four months since the accident. Bryce may not be conscious yet, but I absolutely believe God continues to be in full control of this situation!

Bryce had another good day today. His therapies went well, he did not have any brain storms, and he looked comfortable most of the day.

I played the *Star Wars* theme song a few times for Bryce today. Since Star Wars is his favorite movie, I was hoping it might spark something in him.

He is also a big Yoda fan, so we bought him a large stuffed Yoda last weekend for Valentine's Day. Today I was holding it up in front of Bryce's open eyes, while the music was playing. I hope these familiar things bring him comfort.

Tomorrow Bryce will have his wisdom teeth removed. I have met the oral surgeon. He is a kind, compassionate man, and he has many years of experience under his belt.

Facebook Update: Thursday 2/14/13, 3:00 p.m.

Bryce is resting peacefully and I was able to see him for a few minutes in recovery. The oral surgery took longer than expected, but everything went smoothly.

Thank you for your prayers today. They have been answered.

Love, Cathy

Facebook Update: Friday 2/15/13

The oral surgeon told me he had to cut into and shave the bone areas around each of Bryce's four wisdom teeth. It's no wonder his face is so swollen! He looks like he feels miserable.

Bryce had five active duty Air Force visitors today. They were from Langley AFB 633 Medical Support Squadron. It was so nice of them to check on Bryce again, to make sure we have everything we need, and to be a great support for me too. Thank you, Langley AFB family!

Facebook Update: Sunday 2/17/13

I was able to go to church today. Boy oh boy, did it do wonders for my attitude, outlook, and soul! I sat in the second row. The Lord knows if I sit too far back, I'm unable to focus on the Word of God being spoken because I am way too busy people watching.

It was so wonderful to sing, let go of my worries and stresses, and ultimately fill up my inner tank with all the things God wanted me to receive. I have decided to do this every Sunday while I'm here, and I won't allow myself to feel guilty that I am missing time with Bryce.

I've realized that when I step away and refuel, I have more hope, faith, and joy to actually pass on and share with Bryce.

Pastor Keith Hill from St. Giles Presbyterian Church came to see Bryce this afternoon. He anointed him with oil and together we prayed that God would touch, fully restore, and heal Bryce!

Of course, I don't know what this healing might look like. But I do believe one hundred percent that God knows exactly what Bryce needs.

As his Momma, I can tell you that I love Bryce more than I am able to type in words. I want him to be fully healed here and now. With that said, I also know that God, his Creator, loves him even more than I am capable. I fully trust Him to work out His perfect plan for Bryce's life.

Thank you!

Love, Cathy

Facebook Update: Tuesday 2/19/13

Bryce's mouth is continuing to heal nicely. Some have wondered why we would allow them to take out his wisdom teeth at such a time as this. Well, they were causing him pain all the way back in September of 2012. He was already scheduled to get them out months ago in Japan. We are hoping that with them no longer causing him pain, it might possibly help stop some of his brain storming.

One other note, Bryce can't swallow yet, so it was much safer to go ahead and remove them here in the hospital, where he can be suctioned and monitored very closely by experts.

Facebook Update: Wednesday 2/20/13

I spent time decorating Bryce's hospital room for St. Patrick's Day. I know it's early, but St Patrick's is his favorite holiday! There are paper shamrocks covering the walls, plastic decorations clinging to the windows and mirrors, and even more St Patrick's Day goodies scattered all around.

If you know Bryce, I'm sure you can picture him right now in your mind wearing one of his many "Lucky Irish" or "Kiss Me, I'm Irish" green T-shirts. We always laughed because he wore these favorite T-shirts all year long.

Today I dressed Bryce in his favorite "lucky T-shirt." This is the same shirt he was wearing exactly one year ago, when he came home from Osan, Korea. He was on leave for a couple weeks before reporting to his next duty station in Misawa, Japan.

God is so good to us! I'm praying for a miraculous healing today, in Jesus' Name, Amen!

Love, Cathy

Life Offline

Well, Bryce's healing did not happen on this date as I had expected. Ever since December 13 when I heard that voice say, "I will heal him in seventy days," I had completely believed Bryce would be miraculously healed on February 21. I even told Dr. Pai and a few others on the medical team about the voice I heard.

Who knows what they thought of me now? Hopefully they didn't think I was nuts!

I had never doubted God's ability to heal Bryce. At the same time, I was heartbroken Bryce's healing didn't happen on this day. I was also confused as to why I even heard that voice. I heard it out loud, perfectly clear, and understood it instantly. I didn't know if that meant I was mentally cracking up or if God changed His mind.

I didn't know what to think. I prayed that night, "Father God, please continue to do Your work in this situation. Please continue to give me hope, strength, and courage. Please help me, and help Bryce, get better. Amen"

Chapter Nineteen

Walking by Faith, Not by Sight

Facebook Update: Friday 2/22/13

Thank you for continuing to pray boldly with me for Bryce's healing! Even though we have not seen a healing miracle with our physical eyes yet, please know that God hears every cry, every plea, and every request. None of this is a waste of time or goes unheard.

God has a perfect plan for Bryce, and for each of us! We may not always understand what it is when we are walking through tough times, but He knows! He loves us and wants us to trust Him completely!

So that is what I am choosing to do! I choose to keep trusting God every second of this journey. Regardless of the human results we see, or don't see, He remains God and He remains good!

Facebook Update: Monday 2/25/13

Today has been a long, hard day! Bryce is so full of tone and spasticity issues, he never got a break from the repeated, rhythmic, painful cramping.

I can't stand seeing Bryce's body going through these horrible motions, over and over again. As his Momma, I am having a difficult time knowing I can't do anything to make these storms stop! I also can't imagine how horrible it must be for Bryce.

His doctors can't say for certain whether Bryce has the cognitive ability to understand what is happening to his body, or the ability to experience pain. This is the only time I allow myself to hope he does not know what is happening to him. It's just too painful to think Bryce may be stuck inside of himself, alone, suffering in constant pain, and have no way to make it all stop.

I am praying and begging God for relief! I know full well God has not forgotten him, but my flesh is weak and I want my healthy Bryce back now!

Life Offline

On this day we filed an official inquiry with our state senator in regard to Bryce's accident investigation and "line of duty" determination. Four and a half months after the accident we continued to wait for answers to our many questions. We still had no concrete answers as to what happened to Bryce on the afternoon of October 13, 2012. Was he speeding or being reckless? Did he swerve to miss an animal? Or was it simply a case of a young, inexperienced driver on unfamiliar roads?

We also requested an official explanation as to why he was left to aspirate on the blood in his lungs before and after the medics arrived. We wanted to know why he was not flown to the trauma hospital, especially after suffering such horrific injuries and remaining unconscious the entire time.

Another question: why was Bryce not intubated on the way to the base hospital? And why did it take three intubation attempts to get the optimum levels of oxygen to Bryce's brain? We didn't understand what went wrong. We wanted to know what happened to our son.

We felt unheard, helpless, and afraid. For me personally, after having so much to deal with already, I felt like I was choking and it was becoming harder to breathe. We could only hope and pray that our inquiry would bring answers soon.

Facebook Update: Thursday 2/28/13

It's been great having my husband here in the hospital with me this week. He has been learning all kinds of caretaking techniques and is doing a fantastic job. We have a long list of things we must both do in front of the expert nurses, and then they check them off the list. We are doing everything from crushing medications and inserting them into his stomach PEG feeding tube to using the lifts to get him in and out of his bed or wheelchair.

We are still trying to decide what we will be doing once we leave here. We have a couple of options before us. I will let you know when we make our final decision.

Thank you for your love, prayers, and support!

Love, Cathy

We learned that many people had come to faith in Jesus as a result of what they read on the Facebook prayer page. People would write, "Your family is so inspirational... Wow... What a great example of God's grace!"

I would read this and think, "You don't even know that my husband thinks our marriage is a fraud. Or that I'm gaining a bunch of extra pounds. Or that I secretly started smoking cigarettes. You don't realize that I go to bed and ask God if He is punishing me for getting pregnant with Bryce outside of wedlock." I actually wondered if that's why He allowed this to happen to Bryce—because of my sins. My life felt like it stopped in a lot of ways. I either felt guilty to be going on without Bryce, or felt so sad that this had happened.

Someone wrote on the Facebook page, "Make sure you stay present and deal with this grief. You don't want your daughter to lose her brother, and then her Mom. You don't want your husband to lose his son, and then his wife."

When our family was together physically, often we did not seem to be emotionally connected. At the end of the day, I knew I loved God, and I was going to trust Him to help me—and also Jim and Madison—to get through this with our faith and sanity intact.

MARCH

Facebook Update: Friday 3/1/13

During physical therapy, Bryce walked 1,000 steps in twenty minutes on that cool Erigo walking machine. Walking 1,000 steps in twenty minutes may not normally be something people brag about, but since Bryce is not even conscious yet, we think its amazing progress!

Facebook Update: Saturday 3/2/13

Some days are just hard and it's easy to feel overwhelmed and wish there was a safe place to run and hide. I think these feelings are normal at times, and I'm thankful we have someone to run to for help.

I'm continuing to believe God's Word.

Psalm 46:1b (CSB)
"God is our refuge and strength, a helper who is always found in times of trouble."

Specific prayer requests:

1. For God to have mercy and compassion on Bryce, comforting and protecting him around the clock.

2. For God to have mercy and compassion on our family.

3. For God to help each of us stay upright and on course, as we walk through this difficult season.

Thank you so much for staying, praying, and believing!

Love, Cathy

Life Offline

Jim and Madison received a large shipment containing multiple cardboard boxes full of Bryce's belongings from Japan. Jim took a quick peek inside each box and then decided to put them away until we would have more time to go through them together. The contents represented Bryce's life and dreams. I was grateful his possessions made it home safely, but at the same time it broke my heart. The next day we received a gift and encouraging letter from a military family serving in Misawa.

"Because of your unshakable FAITH, God is going to move this mountain and give you guys a healing for Bryce in JESUS NAME! I also believe that Bryce and you guys are spreading HIS word ALL OVER THE WORLD and that God is using you guys and the whole world is going to experience this miraculous miracle right before their eyes.

I really feel led to tell you that you should write a book, thanking Him, like you already have, in advance for his many miracles.

Carmen"

I continue to notice little changes in Bryce and believe he is slowly waking up and being healed. His eyes are very alive at times, and I can sense he is in there.

I believe he recognizes my voice, my hugs, and my kisses. Sometimes when I am talking to others, he stretches his neck out a little, and turns his head sideways. To me, it seems like he is doing everything possible to eavesdrop on my words.

I really notice this when I am talking to Jim or Madison on the phone. He seems to sit up in bed a little higher and appears to be listening in on my conversations (lol).

Don't worry, I don't talk about anything that would cause him stress or worry in his presence. I do think it's a good sign though, that it seems like he is able to stop his uncontrollable reflexive movements and somehow fully relax enough to sit back and listen in on my conversations.

I guess it's true what they say, "the apple doesn't fall far from the tree."

Facebook Update: Friday 3/8/13

The baclofen pump has been placed and it is operating properly. The surgeon was also able to tap the shunt in Bryce's brain and it is functioning properly as well. Thank you for your continued prayers for my sweet son.

God is so good! He is the Great Physician.

Love, Cathy

Facebook Update: Saturday 3/9/13, 9:00 p.m.

Bryce is continuing to recover and heal from his surgery. The pump medication is set on the lowest setting for now, so we are not seeing much relief with Bryce's spasticity and tone issues yet. Early next week they will raise the baclofen dosage on the pump and lower the oral baclofen given through his PEG tube. Hopefully we will see some improvement when this happens.

Luke 1:37 (NLT)

"For nothing is impossible with God."

Thank you for praying with me!

Love, Cathy

Life Offline

I couldn't help but wonder what affect all the surgeries Bryce had since his accident were having on his brain. I fully trusted the medical professionals making these decisions and knew each procedure performed was meant to help Bryce further heal. But I also knew it was a risk every time he was placed under anesthesia and intubated. This was just one of those moments where I needed to keep walking forward, one day at a time, placing my complete faith and trust in God to protect Bryce.

Facebook Update: Tuesday 3/12/13

I was reading in the book of Romans today, and I was again comforted that nothing can separate Bryce from the love of God, including any troubles or circumstances he faces in this life, not even a brain injury or semi-consciousness. That is so like God!

Romans 8:38-39 (GNT)
"For I am certain that nothing can separate us from his love: neither death nor life, neither angels nor other heavenly rulers or powers, neither the present nor the future, neither the world above nor the world below—there is nothing in all creation that will ever be able to separate us from the love of God which is ours through Christ Jesus our Lord."

Thank you, Prayer Warriors!

Love, Cathy

Chapter Twenty

Living on a Prayer

Facebook Update: Wednesday 3/13/13

Today is exactly five months since Bryce's accident. I am so thankful he is still here with us, and I'm also thankful for the many miracles we have already witnessed in his recovery.

The best part of his day happened around 3:30 p.m.

Our daughter Madison has been on a City of Monroe Youth Council trip to Washington DC since last Friday. Today they were on their way home and passing through Richmond. It was so cool! Madison was sound asleep on the bus when they pulled into the hospital parking lot. They let me board the bus, walk all the way to the back where she was sleeping, tap her on the shoulder, and say, "Hello." Poor kid! She saw me, then cried and cried.

After all the tears and some of the shock wore off, she was so happy to see me and Bryce! Everyone from the bus joined us! It was just an amazing and special time!

Our mayor, Bobby Kilgore, presented Bryce with an official City of Monroe, NC, pin. A whole lot of love and tears filled Bryce's room as the mayor lifted up a beautiful prayer.

Life Offline

I couldn't imagine how tough it was to be in Madison's shoes at that time. Her life was completely flipped upside down. She had never been separated from me outside of a weeklong trip, and I had been gone from home since October. She worried about her brother in the fight for his life and wished none of this ever happened.

Even so, she had to step up her game and take on much more responsibility at home with chores, cooking and laundry. In addition to the normal pressures of schoolwork and homework, she also had friends and teachers who knew personal information about her family's daily struggles.

My heart hurt for Madison and I wanted to protect her from all of this. Every day I prayed that she would be surrounded by caring and compassionate individuals, helping her to not feel afraid or lonely.

I know God allows situations to happen in our lives for a purpose. Even if we don't understand all of the whys, He is faithful in turning the ashes to beauty if we just hold on, trust Him, and allow Him to work. I had to trust God to heal Madison's broken heart.

Facebook Update: Thursday 3/14/13

There have been no connections in the last few days. This is most likely because of the extra toll his body has gone through going under the anesthesia.

His doctors went up a little bit on his baclofen pump dosage yesterday, but it is not making much of a difference. He will need to slowly go up quite a bit more over the next couple of weeks.

Today the social worker and director met with me to discuss discharge plans. I'm not angry or upset. I realize they must keep their beds open for other patients who are making bigger gains than Bryce.

With all that said, for me change is tough, and the unknown is scary. Unfortunately, my being afraid will not stop the changes or the unknown from happening. In order to feel any peace at all, I must continue to walk forward, trust God, pray for mercy, and believe everything will work together for Bryce's good.

After all, Bryce belongs to God.

Facebook Update: Saturday 3/16/13, 8:45 p.m.

Today we were blessed with a visit from twelve Air Force AMMO Chiefs. The group had switched their quarterly meeting to Richmond, Virginia, just so they could come see Bryce and support our family. They blessed our family with a monetary gift to help us during this rough time. Thank you so much for loving and blessing us, ACA!

Love, Cathy

Life Offline

One of the VA hospital barbers gave me a lesson on how to properly cut Bryce's hair. I told him about our impending discharge, and he understood that it will be tough for me to bring Bryce to a barbershop once we moved home. He took time to show me the best men's hair cutting tools and shared where I can get them for a fair price. What a great guy!

Facebook Update: Sunday 3/17/13

Happy St Patrick's Day! This day has always been a favorite for Bryce. I made sure he wore his special shamrock green "Lucky Shirt" today, and then I pushed him in his tilted-back wheelchair outside to enjoy the cool fresh air.

Today was a good health day. It was also a day of peace for the both of us. I'm noticing that Bryce doesn't make as much noise. Before the baclofen pump, he used to moan in pain quite a bit; now there is silence. Thank you, Father God, for giving Bryce peace!

This is a great verse I read today.

Psalm 3:5 (NLT)
"I lay down and slept, yet I woke up in safety, for the Lord was watching over me."

Thank you.

Love, Cathy

Today I saw a little spark in Bryce that leads me to believe he is getting closer to waking up. The connection was there. I felt it, I recognized it, and I believe it without a shadow of doubt!

Dear Prayer Warriors, we are getting closer to the miraculous day Bryce will wake up. I sure hope you believe in miraculous recoveries too. Just a tiny mustard seed of faith is all we need. I believe!

Matthew 17:20 (GNT)

"I assure you that if you have faith as big as a mustard seed, you can say to this hill, 'Go from here to there!' and it will go. You could do anything!"

Thank you!

Love, Cathy

Life Offline

I have a mustard seed that I carry inside my wallet. I'm not sure if most people realize just how small they are. I was surprised the first time I laid eyes on that tiny seed. I believe I have more faith inside of me than one of those tiny little mustard seeds!

Yet, there we were, still waiting for a miraculous healing for Bryce. It was hard to sit and wait. It was also difficult to not overthink why his healing hadn't come yet. I kept thinking of anything I could do, or say, or pray to be good enough in God's eyes so He would want to heal Bryce.

There were some days I just wanted to move far away from everyone and everything I knew. I felt so overwhelmed with worry, fear, and anxiety. I wondered what would happen to Bryce and our family when all was said and done.

I hated that I had a desire to run, to escape. I was always asking God for more peace, to keep calm and carry on. Then at some point I started to realize that maybe it wasn't about me being good enough, Bryce being good enough, or any of us being good enough for God to miraculously heal him. I came to the conclusion that I simply needed to place my full trust in Him, knowing He is the One that can work all things together for our good. I came to the place where His perfect will was all I wanted. It was the one thing I knew I could depend upon.

Facebook Update: Tuesday 3/19/13

Today I decorated Bryce's hospital room for Easter. I thought how strange it would be for Bryce to wake up and see Easter decorations all around him, especially since he fell asleep in the middle of October! I'm glad I will be here to answer all of his questions!

Thank you!

Love, Cathy

Facebook Update: Wednesday 3/20/13

Today was an off day. I noticed early on Bryce seemed to have much more tone and spasticity issues than he has had since his baclofen pump surgery. By this afternoon, he was moaning nonstop.

He was clearly showing signs of brain storming, but his doctor didn't wait until it was full blown to give him a shot of relief medication. It was clear to all of us Bryce was extremely uncomfortable and needed a break from the pain.

Today's issue may have been a result of an increase in medication used to try and wake Bryce up. They will lower the dose tomorrow and see if it helps.

Facebook Update: Thursday 3/21/13

Bryce's doctors are slowly, but steadily, increasing his baclofen dose via the pump, while coming down on the oral dose. I can see a big difference in his tone and spasticity. I am praising God for this good report!

Our time is running out here at the VA Polytrauma. Unless Bryce wakes up, his care will end here in another week or two. We were given a civilian care facility option to send Bryce to, but our family has no peace with that decision.

So the great news is that Bryce and I will be going home to our family in the very near future!

We are turning our living room into a hospital room for Bryce. Jim is working hard to get things ready for us. He is even installing a large standby generator. Bryce is unable to swallow, so we cannot take the chance of him needing suctioning or other lifesaving treatment and not be able to help him during a power outage. We are so blessed that Jim is an electrician.

The wheelchair ramp builders came to our home today. We're hoping to get a ramp built for Bryce in the near future.

Jim and Madison are both excited to have us home! They have both sacrificed a lot in the last one hundred fifty-nine days.

Facebook Update: Friday 3/22/13

I have been giddy all day. Peace and happiness has been welling up inside and overflowing out of me. Without any extra effort on my part, I have been singing praise songs and humming happy tunes out loud. I would say my hope, joy, and faith tanks are completely filled to the brim!

I wish I could tell you Bryce officially woke up today, but that has not happened yet. I just sense strongly that something awesome is getting ready to happen in this eleventh hour!

God is in this! Believe me! At a time when everything is so up in the air, I would normally be dreading the changes getting ready to happen, and yet here I am feeling super excited about the future! It's the strangest, coolest feeling in the world!

I sure hope you all don't think I've finally snapped under the pressure, because I'm certain that is not the case. This is the peace of God falling afresh on me.

Our God is an awesome God!

Love, Cathy

Facebook Update: Saturday 3/23/13

This is the best day Bryce has had since October 13, 2012. I'm seeing more and more signs of awareness in Bryce. Typically, these signs show up in very small windows, and the rest of the day there is nothing much to report. Well, the super cool news is that these windows seem to be getting bigger.

Today I saw a small handful of windows with signs of awareness in Bryce. I also felt quite a few connections, and I truly believe with all my heart, mind, and soul, Bryce is beginning to wake up!

I don't have all the answers or know anything for sure, but I plan to run all of my experiences and thoughts by the medical professionals on Monday, to see what they think.

Medically speaking, they are expecting Bryce to have severe deficits when he does wake up. Faith speaking, I am expecting Bryce to be miraculously healed by God. Even now, there are thousands of prayer warriors interceding for this.

Thank you.

Love, Cathy

This morning I was able to sit down with Dr. Pai and tell him about all the connections and windows of awareness I have been recently seeing in Bryce. He was genuinely excited with me, and for Bryce, with what I am seeing.

He then helped me to understand better, from a doctor's point of view, how the healing process tends to look for patients such as Bryce, who have suffered a catastrophic layered traumatic brain injury.

The big news of the day, medically speaking, is that these types of layered brain injuries typically take many years to heal, if ever. The more severe the brain trauma and injury, the less chance there is for any recovery. For Bryce to wake up and have his life back, we need a miracle from God.

When I showed him my weekend video clips of Bryce, I was expecting to hear, "Wow, looks like he is waking up. Let's enroll him in our traumatic brain injury rehabilitation program immediately!" That's not what happened.

All of the connections I'm sensing with Bryce are positive and show that he is in there. At the same time, he needs to be consistent and be able to connect with us for hours, every day, and not just a few seconds here and there. The bottom line is Bryce needs healing, time, and a touch from God to work through these multiple layers.

If I may be blunt with you all, I completely get it as far as all the medical information and the scientific realities we face. I also appreciate the amazing men and women here that dedicate their lives to helping our loved ones recover from injuries and illnesses.

I also totally get it that our God is a big God, and He can heal Bryce and change his circumstances in an instant. My hope and faith will remain as strong as ever in our loving God, the Great Physician.

Thank you for praying!

Love, Cathy

Chapter Twenty-One

Screaming Loudly on the Inside

I was so thankful for Dr. Pai. I remembered the first time I saw his name was in Hawaii when Bryce's neurosurgeon gave me the great news that Bryce had been accepted in to a TBI emerging consciousness program in Virginia. When I looked at the approved paperwork, I saw the words, "Accepting Physician: Dr. Ajit Pai." I decided right then and there that I really liked this doctor! He was, after all, the reason Bryce was allowed to come to this top-notch facility.

Seeing him almost every day and having many opportunities to get to know him better, I grew to love and respect this doctor! How could we not love someone so willing to try everything to heal Bryce? Dr. Pai is a brilliant, compassionate man. His door was always open for me. If it weren't for this amazing doctor and his magnificent team, I'm sure I would have crashed and burned by this point.

Facebook Update: Tuesday 3/26/13

Bryce and I will be going home on April 10. My forty-sixth birthday is on April 11. I was thinking of how great it will be once we're all back home, getting to sleep in my own bed again, and to have all of us under the same roof. It will be the best birthday present ever!

Facebook Update: Wednesday 3/27/13

I was so upset today when Bryce's physical therapist told me he had a condition called "drop foot," which is the inability to lift the front part of the foot due to weakness or paralysis of the muscles that lift the foot. As a result, Bryce will not be able to walk again, even if he ever emerges.

This news was "off the charts" devastating. It seemed so much more permanent of a condition than a coma. I was crying hysterically, thinking that all hope was fading fast. The therapist said that Bryce could undergo many surgeries in an attempt to help the problem someday, but that it would not be considered until after he has emerged.

I had the sickest feelings inside, like we were running out of time. These were horrible moments to add to the already horrible season we were living.

Facebook Update: Thursday 3/28/13

Today we had two wonderful visitors from Langley Air Force Base: Sergeant Heitzenroeder and Sergeant Zeigler. They tried their best to wake Bryce up AMMO style! They did an "AMMO call" and an "AMMO coin check."

Not only did they have my full attention, but I think they had Bryce's too. The minute they walked into the hospital room, Bryce's eyes seemed to scan back and forth, and he looked like he was seeing their uniforms. Even their voices seemed to catch his attention. It was so awesome!

I love our AMMO family! Every time I see an AMMO troop walk through Bryce's hospital room door I feel a huge wave of pride, safety, and comfort. It takes all my strength to not begin weeping and smothering them with AMMO Momma hugs and kisses. Thank you AMMO family!

Life Offline

An AMMO call is a loud cheer that everyone says together. One person hollers out, "AMMO!" and everyone collectively yells back, "AMMO!" It's for morale.

An AMMO challenge coin is a decorative coin, usually with a picture of some type of munition. Every AMMO troop receives a challenge coin when they graduate Munitions Tech School. They can be purchased, but the best way to receive one is to earn it for a job well done.

Once AMMO, always AMMO! Even after transitioning from active duty to veteran status, many still keep an AMMO coin in their pocket.

The AMMO coin check is when an AMMO troop is "challenged" by another who has taken his coin out of his pocket and drops it onto a hard surface. The other AMMO troop is expected to "meet the challenge" by pulling their own AMMO coin out of their pocket and dropping it down as well. If they are caught without their coin, they are expected to buy the challenger a beverage of their choice. If they are able to drop their coin, then the initiator must buy the beverage.

It is wonderful to have Jim and Madison safe and sound in Richmond. Having them close enough to kiss and hug makes everything a little better. Thank you, Father, for blessing me with such a great family!

Bryce has been wiped out all day. He was so tired, much more than usual, and just seemed different to me. He also had another brain storm late this afternoon.

Jim, Madison, and I went to a special Armed Forces Dinner tonight in the hospital. The food, fellowship, and entertainment were exceptional! I would like to give a special shout out to the volunteers who worked hard to make it happen.

Life Offline

I was shocked on this day when one of the resident doctors told me Bryce's brain was shrinking. I never realized this could happen. I was at the nurse's desk, and the resident was giving me an update on Bryce, specifically telling me how Bryce is continuing to lose even more function, going backward instead of forward.

When he told me this, I said, "Well he wasn't doing this before. Why is he doing it now?"

He looked at me and said very matter-of-factly, "Well you know his brain is shrinking, right?"

I said, "What?"

He repeated, "His brain is shrinking."

At this point I could feel myself beginning to flip out on the inside. "What do you mean his brain is shrinking?"

"Imagine if more than half of your brain cells were injured, and they're dead now," he explained. "They are all holding space inside your skull. So now the injured ones that have died begin to shrivel up and the body reabsorbs them. So those areas are basically replaced with fluid and holes throughout the brain. Then the brain shrinks."

Bryce's brain, which had been like a swollen superball in Japan, with the hydrocephalus and intracranial pressure building, was now a shriveling mass of once stretched out and damaged brain cells that were now dead. His brain was basically caving in on itself.

Of course, he still had some healthy brain cells left, but the damage spread throughout his patch-filled brain. When I heard that I couldn't help but think, "There is no hope. What are we doing?"

The reality was that Bryce's brain was deteriorating as we watched helplessly.

Facebook Update: Saturday 3/30/13

Bryce had an absolutely beautiful visitor today, Rosemary Willis, Miss Virginia, 2012. It's a neat story how she ended up here at the Richmond VA. A wounded warrior Purple Heart recipient, Franz Walkup, and his lovely wife, Shannon Walkup, who have become dear friends of ours, met Miss America up at Walter Reed last month. During their visit, they told Miss America about Bryce recovering here in Richmond, and right then and there, she called Miss Virginia on her cell phone and asked her to come pay Bryce a visit.

How cool are all of these people?

Miss Virginia, along with a group of other crowned beauties, traveled to the Richmond VA to visit all of the wounded warriors and veterans. These women are beautiful both on the inside and the outside.

We took plenty of pictures for Bryce to see later. I thought for sure he would wake up surrounded by all those gorgeous young ladies. He will be kicking himself when he sees the photos someday.

Love, Cathy

Facebook Update: Sunday 3/31/13

Happy Easter, faithful Prayer Warriors! God is so awesome! He gave our family a sneak peek at the healing He has begun inside Bryce!

Here's the story:

Madison and I were loudly laughing about something that had happened and all of a sudden Bryce began smiling. The more we laughed, the more he smiled. We were all amazed! It lasted for about three minutes and was just enough time for us to get a nurse in his room to take our family Easter photo for 2013.

Our God is great! With His healing touch, I believe these precious windows of awareness will keep coming, and eventually get longer and longer!

Thank you for praying and believing with me!

Love, Cathy

APRIL

Madison and I took Bryce outside for a little while this afternoon to get some fresh air and enjoy the beautiful spring weather.

Tonight Bryce fell right to sleep after our evening routine of tender loving prayer and care. Madison and I then stood close to him, watching him sleep. We hugged each other as we silently shared the sweet, and also bittersweet, reality of the moment.

Our hope continues to be in the Lord! We believe He has a great plan!

Life Offline

Anxiety was a constant battle because I could not turn off my thoughts. I was sleep deprived due to fear and worry about the "line of duty" determination.

I guess it was just the protective "Momma Bear" in me. I know it probably seemed strange that I would worry about anything other than Bryce's physical healing at this point, but protecting his character, integrity, and reputation were also important to me. I wanted the world to know Bryce was an intelligent, trustworthy, amazing young man. He had a beautiful and enormous heart, and I would have trusted him with my life. He was a great son, brother, and friend!

Facebook Update: Tuesday 4/2/13

Tonight I want to share with you that none of this is easy. None of it! Some people think I am strong or inspirational, but the truth is every single day I have to recommit myself to trusting God to endure another day. It's as simple as that.

I wake up feeling overwhelmed, weak, afraid, sad, and lonely, with great loss and so much heartache. I usually pull the covers over my head wanting to hide. Then I cry out to God for help and He is always there for me. Our God is so faithful!

Madison and I are enjoying our special time together. I am so thankful she is here with me and Bryce.

We left the hospital for a few hours today in search of a prom dress. We found a vintage store close by. Madison picked out the perfect dress for her "Old Hollywood" themed prom.

You can probably imagine how much fun she had trying on all the elegant dresses, hats, gloves, and shoes. It was wonderful to see her so happy, and I'm glad she has something exciting to look forward to. She is a precious young lady and I am blessed to be her Momma.

Facebook Update: Wednesday 4/3/13

I realized today that I don't like to wait. When I started thinking about why I don't like to wait, I decided that most likely it's because I worry I might not get what it is that I am waiting for. Somehow if I'm actively trying to rush God, or even people, I feel much safer, thinking I'm going to get all my needs met.

I know in my heart this is not the way faith works, and I shouldn't be running around behind the scenes, forcing my agenda to get what I want. I guess I need to work on trusting God more, and wait for Him to move on our behalf.

I asked myself, if I knew for sure that I would get exactly what I wanted, would I still hate having to wait for it?

My honest answer was no. I don't think I would mind waiting if I could always control the outcome and ensure that I get the goods at the other end of the line.

Wow. I hadn't even realized until today how selfish my intentions of waiting on God to heal my son have been. It may be understandable to be desperate and selfish in this situation, but it is not who I want to be.

I want to be a Momma that seeks and trusts the Lord, regardless of the outcome. It's not that I don't want to see Bryce restored immediately to good health, but I know God's plans are better than anything I can conjure up. He loves Bryce, me, our family, and every one of you reading this way more than we can dream or imagine.

Life Offline

The military Brass told me Sarah couldn't remember anything that happened a week or two before the accident. Bryce's doctor said that her memory of that time will probably never come back. The brain blocks these memories to protect the patient. They are buried forever in one's subconscious.

At the same time, the military investigators were waiting for her to get better so she could tell them exactly what happened before they would rule on Bryce's "line of duty" determination.

Usually the line of duty determination is completed within six months, but without her memory of the details, it was becoming evident to us, the military would never know exactly what happened. How long would we have to wait for their decision?

Facebook Update: Friday 4/5/13

Madison and I have had a wonderful time together this week. She is so inspiring and amazing. Her heart is pure gold. Thank you Lord for blessing me with such a sweet daughter!

Jim will be arriving here in Richmond tomorrow, then driving back home with Madison on Sunday.

Specific prayer request:

For God to help our family to not crumble or become a statistic under all this stress, but instead change each of us for the better.

Thank you for your continued prayers!

Love, Cathy

We had been hoping everything would work out and that Bryce would just wake up, but each time we got our hopes up, we were faced with another setback. The reality of Bryce's condition finally became clear when Dr. Pai showed Jim and me an MRI that confirmed that Bryce's brain was actually dissolving. They showed us several MRI images, and in all of them we saw black spots the size of a quarter. "What are these black spots?" Jim asked. "They weren't there on the earlier MRIs."

Dr. Pai explained that Bryce's brain was dissolving the injured areas. The brain did what it could to heal itself and reroute the learning to different areas, but was unsuccessful. Because the dead brain cells appeared to be foreign, the body attacked them like white cells go after germs. The areas in Bryce's brain that were not working were deteriorating and being expelled and there was nothing they could do.

Facebook Update: Saturday 4/6/13

Jim and Madison took me out to dinner tonight at the historic Jefferson Hotel to celebrate my birthday. My birthday is not until Thursday, April 11, but they go back home tomorrow.

We had a delicious dinner and enjoyed a tour through the hotel. The grand staircase at the Jefferson Hotel is exactly the same as the famous staircase featured in the movie, *Gone with the Wind*. I'm thankful for the wonderful evening out with loved ones.

Life Offline

Things became frustrating when I would tell Jim, "I got Bryce to blink twice today."

And he would say, "Did anyone see it?"

And I would say, "No, but I know it happened because I saw it."

More than once I told him Michael, the speech therapist, saw a possible connection happening too and had documented it in Bryce's medical chart. Jim was happy to hear the report, but closely guarded his emotions and reaction until he could see it for himself.

It got to the point where I felt like the little boy who cried wolf. Whenever I sensed a connection with Bryce, I would get so excited about it and share it with everyone, from family to Facebook to the all of the medical staff. Occasionally, Dr. Pai caught a glimpse of what I was seeing, but they were never consistent or purposeful actions.

Each time Jim and Madison came to visit, they would talk to Bryce, touch him, and interact with him, trying to help him make a connection, but to no avail. Since Jim and Madison never witnessed these tiny glimpses of the "old Bryce," I don't know if they believed me or thought I was just wishful thinking. I clearly remember seeing the doubt and disappointment on their faces though. It broke my heart. I wanted them to witness those moments of connection too, but it didn't happen.

Facebook Update: Monday 4/8/13

I have been looking at pictures of the kids from a long time ago. Madison sent them to me last night. It's bittersweet to see these photos. Of course they are cute, but at the same time, as a parent you look back and wish you could somehow protect your kids from all pain, harm and danger.

This reality led me to start thinking about bigger things. I wonder if this is how God feels about us when we end up in situations that are dangerous, causing us spiritual, emotional, or physical pain. Seeing, feeling, and experiencing these things from a parent's perspective sure makes me want to try harder to stay within the bounds God has set for me.

Facebook Update: Tuesday 4/9/13

Bryce has now been up on the Erigo walking machine a total of twenty-seven times. The machine is still doing one hundred percent of the work for him as he is tightly strapped in, but it is definitely helping his body stretch and become healthier as he goes along for the ride.

They have slowly increased the number of steps, and today he walked over 1,500! I'm completely blown away by today's technology! Just imagine, a person in a semiconscious state walking over 1,500 steps! How cool is that?

Facebook Update: Wednesday 4/10/13

Today has been rough.

Bryce had an appointment with the chief of ophthalmology and another optometrist today.

Together, they diagnosed Bryce to be blind in both of his eyes. His condition is called cortical visual impairment, which is blindness in the brain. They said he has nerve damage that is permanent.

I am not sure what to do about this. I am not sure how exactly to handle it. I need time to pray and process.

Physically they say my baby is now blind. It feels like a couple of big scoops of nightmare packed on top of what we already thought was our worst nightmare.

At the same time, I also completely get that our God can fix blindness. He has done this already, and it is written in the Bible.

Love, Cathy

Life Offline

I was watching Bryce getting worse as the days went by. His body curled, he moaned, and I didn't know if he was suffering. In tears, I begged for more medication, so he could peacefully sleep. But then more medication would not help him to wake up. I started to realize just how horrible Bryce's quality of life really was! I WAS SCREAMING LOUDLY ON THE INSIDE!

I also received this information:

"The American Academy of Neurology states that of the adults in a persistent vegetative state for three months after brain trauma, 35 percent will die within a year after the injury. Another 30 percent will go into a permanent vegetative state, 19 percent will recover with severe disabilities, and 16 percent will recover with a moderate or minimal disability.

"If they remain in a persistent vegetative state for six months, 32 percent will die, 52 percent will go on to a permanent vegetative state, 12 percent will recover with severe disabilities, and 4 percent will recover with moderate or minimal disability.

"Nontraumatic brain damage markedly decreases the chance of any recovery. After six months, no adults who remain in that state recover."

Bryce had suffered multiple layers of traumatic and nontraumatic brain injuries. His brain had also shrunk. All of his injured and now dead brain cells had been slowly reabsorbed back into his body, leaving gaping black spaces on the scans where his healthy brain was once visible.

For six months, the doctors have tried everything they could think of to help him wake up, and now I had to face the reality of that last sentence: "After six months, no adults who remain in that state recover."

This reality brought me so much sadness, and yet it also caused me to question EVERYTHING!

What are we doing? What would Bryce want?

I prayed, "Lord God, please help us! I know Bryce would hate having to live locked inside himself without the ability to think or function, only feeling pain! This is a horrific quality of life! I can't imagine having to live this way! My poor Bryce! Please give us wisdom Father!"

Chapter Twenty-Two

Honoring Bryce's Wishes

Facebook Update: Thursday 4/11/13

Thank you all for the wonderful "Happy Birthday" messages! They are very sweet.

Bryce's doctors and medical team came in to his room early this morning during their rounds and surprised me with a "Happy Birthday" serenade! It was so nice of them to take time out of their busy schedules to spend a few minutes with me.

Bryce seemed to be in pain most of the day. He rhythmically cramped over and over, all day long.

His doctor tried a new medication this morning to see if it would bring relief, but unfortunately it didn't help.

By late this afternoon he was still having the same issues, so his doctor ordered a CT scan of his brain. They did it tonight. I should hear the results tomorrow.

Love, Cathy

Life Offline

I decided it was time to talk to Dr. Pai about Bryce's quality of life. He had been moaning and storming for hours. I wanted him to give Bryce more pain medication so he could rest. But the doctor was convinced Bryce had enough pain medication to be comfortable. He didn't want to continue giving him more because of the affects it would have on his body.

As the day progressed, the moaning and storming continued and I was beyond agitated. Wondering if Bryce was suffering with every passing moment was driving me crazy. The fact that we had just learned Bryce was also blind on top of everything else just added insult to injury. It seemed to be the last nail in the coffin.

Now, for the first time, I was sensing the absolute dread that he was not going to be getting better. Too much was wrong. Too many systems were broken. I remember the panic that had gripped me when I was told that he had drop foot and that he would probably never walk again. That had seemed a million times worse that hearing Bryce had a TBI. I don't know why I always thought he'd be fine someday. I just really believed with all my heart that he would come through all this with a beautiful and miraculous healing.

None of his injuries ever seemed permanent to me. Now the wear and tear on his body was showing up crystal clear, and I felt overwhelmed with sadness and anger. His brain continued to shrink and dissolve. His fingers were twisting and remained tightly clenched. His body was curling into itself. He had to be fitted with boots and braces for his arms and legs to try and keep his extremities from permanently twisting and deteriorating.

Through it all, even as the reality of how bad Bryce's injuries really were was becoming clear, the one thing I consistently did every morning was to put Bryce's glasses on him. I would make sure they were nice and clean so at least he could see what was happening around him. I was comforted thinking that at least my baby could see his surroundings.

When I learned that he was brain blind I just lost it. I was so angry. I felt stupid. I wondered if all the doctors who had taken care of Bryce knew how bad his injuries really were and were just politely waiting for me to finally "get it" myself.

In fairness, they all did tell me his injuries were severe. Somehow I always finished their sentences with, "But our God is good, and nothing is impossible with Him. He can heal Bryce any time He wants." I never allowed myself to think about Bryce's life without a healing touch from God.

But now I was completely overwhelmed with grief and sadness.

Late in the day, Dr. Pai stopped by to check in on us. I told him about the storming and asked if we could give Bryce some stronger pain meds to make the suffering stop. Dr. Pai explained that even though he was storming and moaning, he didn't think Bryce was actually suffering.

He explained that Bryce wasn't likely aware of his own existence, so having the ability to understand he was in pain was probably not even a reality for Bryce. Dr. Pai was confident that Bryce wasn't aware of himself or his surroundings.

Wow. I felt like I'd been hit with a bag of bricks. Bryce did not even know he existed. That was a very serious statement.

"If Bryce doesn't even know he exists, then what are we doing to Bryce? What is his quality of life?"

Dr. Pai listened, and I could tell his heart was broken for me. It was apparent I was finally beginning to understand just how bad things really were for my son. I could feel myself freaking out. Even if he emerges, what kind of life will he have? This is never going to get better. Bryce would hate this. Do we even have any options?"

Dr. Pai looked at me and quietly said, "There are options."

"What do you mean there are options?"

So he came further into the room and sat down in a chair next to me. "There are things that we can do. We usually don't bring it up, but since you have asked, let's discuss them."

"Right now Bryce is sustained by his feeding tube and medical intervention. He cannot eat. He cannot swallow. He cannot pick up food. He doesn't know that he exists. So we are keeping him nourished and keeping his body healthy, but his brain is not getting any better. It's probably not going to get any better."

Then we quietly discussed the options of stopping all further life supporting medical care and instead replacing it with comfort care and pain management. This would keep Bryce comfortable while we allowed him to succumb to his injuries.

I couldn't believe this was even an option. Maybe someone told me and I just wasn't listening or I wasn't open to it. I don't know for sure, but on this day I finally understood that we had options.

There was such a soft, kind tone in Dr. Pai's voice. It was clear to me that he had wanted Bryce to emerge and get better, too. He had literally tried everything medically he could think of to make that happen. Unfortunately, with all the levels of severe TBI Bryce had suffered, it was now nearly impossible that he would ever recover.

"We see a lot of patients," Dr. Pai explained. "Some emerge, and unfortunately some don't. Some families choose to move their loved one to a nursing home, and some choose to take them home."

"By taking Bryce home, do you mean take him home to die?"

"Some people do that, but that can all be handled in a hospital setting as well."

I shared the latest details Jim had given me about modifying our home with Dr. Pai. Just to get Bryce home it would cost at least $350,000, and we had no concrete time frame as to how long it would take to build all that was needed. And then we had no guarantee that Bryce wouldn't die within a month of coming home. It didn't make sense.

"I'm so sorry," Dr. Pai responded. "We don't know how long Bryce will live in this condition."

I was crying because I knew what he was saying was true. "Thank you so much, Dr. Pai."

He responded as if he was my brother. "I'm so sorry."

"I need to talk to Jim about everything we discussed."

"Okay, then why don't we have a family meeting when Jim returns?"

I told him he'd be here for the weekend, and we made plans to sit down and talk about this with Jim.

I called Jim, and the ball started rolling. I thought it would be something that we would take our time to decide. But once this dialogue began, everything happened very quickly.

"I need to talk to you about something really important," I said when I called Jim. "It's something really horrible and I think you're going to be mad at me."

"No, I'm not going to be mad," he replied calmly. "Actually I've been waiting for this call."

His response shocked me.

"Okay, I think it's worse than what you're thinking. You have no idea what I'm going to say. Once I say it, you may think I'm a horrible person and the worst mother in the world."

Again he said, "No, I'm telling you, I've been waiting for this call."

I was wondering if he thought I was going to talk about us getting a divorce or something like that. I said, "It's about Bryce."

"I know, hold on a minute, let me go outside so Madison doesn't hear me talking."

When he got outside I continued. "Bryce has been in so much pain, and well, at least his body autonomically thinks it's in pain, and they wouldn't keep giving him enough medicine today to make it stop. It was so awful. So I had a discussion with Dr. Pai about what our options are, because I am wondering if Bryce has any quality of life. Dr. Pai said we could remove all medication and feeding and allow him to succumb to his injuries."

"I agree," Jim said firmly. "Don't sign any papers though. Don't sign anything."

"I am not going to," I replied.

"I don't want you to have to do that. I will sign them, not you."

That scared me, because Jim really cares about the human life. So I was thinking that he would be really mad at me for even suggesting any of this. But then Jim told me that he believed Bryce was already gone. He felt it was just his shell that we were tending to.

"It's time to honor Bryce's wishes. He would not want to live this way."

I said everything that was in my heart and so did he. It was the beginning of a three-day dialogue that would change all of our lives forever. But I was worried about Madison and how she would feel about this. Jim didn't think we should ask Madison.

"Well, we need to tell her. We need to talk to Madison and let her know what is going on."

We decided to have a family meeting after we discussed things with Dr. Pai.

The next morning, the phone rang, and it was Madison calling from school. If it hadn't been a call to my cell phone with caller ID, I probably would not have realized it was Madison. She was sobbing uncontrollably. Fear instantly gripped me.

When I was finally able to understand what she was saying, I heard her say, "Momma, I heard you and Dad talking on the phone last night."

Oh no! Oh no! Oh no! My heart and thoughts were racing. I was wondering what exactly she heard, how much she heard, and from whom. Did she only hear Dad's side of the conversation? Or had she heard my words too?

Trying to sound as calm as possible, I told her she probably thinks she heard something but not to worry about anything because we would never play God when it comes to Bryce.

"Mom?" It was sort of a painful moan crying out to me.

"Madi, what's wrong?" I said, trying to get her to snap out of it.

Madi admitted that she picked up an extension and overheard our conversation about Bryce's quality of life and she asked me, "Why are we keeping him alive?"

I panicked. "Madi, Madi, no, no, no, don't worry." I cut her right off. "We're not going to do anything. We will never play God."

"Momma, we're already playing God."

Her words pierced my heart. I had never even thought about that. Never did it cross my mind that we were playing God. I certainly didn't want God to be mad at me, so when I heard her words I was stunned.

"I don't know why everybody is so afraid of death," she continued. "Death is natural. We are all going to die. Why are you afraid to let him die, Mom? He's a Christian, and he's going to Heaven. Bryce would be so mad at us. He would hate this."

She used the word hate!

"Wow, Madi, I didn't know you felt that way. I understand. We are going to have a family meeting. Please stop crying. It's going to be okay. We will talk about it."

I was just blown away. Our sweet Madison had more wisdom in her words than I had expected. She is a brave, faith-filled young woman, not afraid to accept reality, nor let go of her big brother. She knew where he was going and believed that place would be a whole lot better for Bryce. She also believed we will see him healthy again in Heaven.

I was shocked and also relieved. I felt sadness and a wave of peace wash over me. We were all being led in the same direction, individually and as a family.

I was thinking, "Oh my gosh, this is really happening. We are letting him go." God brought each of us here, all in different ways, and yet all to the same place.

Facebook Update: Saturday 4/13/13

Today marks the six-month mark since Bryce had his life-changing accident in Japan. Imagine, one hundred and eighty-two long, tough days trying to come back to us.

During this time, I have seen a lot, learned a lot, cried, prayed, waited, begged, pleaded, kicked, screamed, fought, pushed, pulled, advocated, and rallied the troops. I want you to know that I would do it all again!

I also want you to know that I continue to love, trust, and praise our amazing God for sustaining us each day. I'm thankful God continues to keep Bryce safe in the palm of His hand. I am also grateful He has sent us so many faithful prayer warriors to walk this journey with us.

I wish I could turn back time. I wish Bryce was awake. I wish I was home with Jim and Madison. I wish, I wish, I wish. Reality and wishes are two very different places, so I am choosing to keep on trusting God in spite of my desperate Momma wishes.

Life Offline

After much discussion, prayer, education, hugs, and tears, we decided as a family to honor Bryce's wishes that life-sustaining treatment be discontinued. We have seen firsthand that "being alive" and "living life" are two very different realities.

After our decision had been made, Jim said he needed to share something with me. "I want to tell you something. Remember back in December, before Christmas, when our dog Koehler bit the neighbor?"

"Yeah."

"Let me tell you about the vision I saw that day."

I immediately started thinking, "Oh, now what?"

"You and Madi were sitting over by the window, in Bryce's room playing on your iPads. I was sitting in the chair across from Bryce, just looking at him. I saw Bryce sit straight up, and rise through the ceiling tiles."

"What? What happened? What do you mean? Was he smiling? Did he look at you? Did he look at me?"

"Listen to me," Jim said, trying to calm me down.

I continued asking questions. "Was it just his spirit, like on TV? Was he invisible?"

"Listen to me," he repeated. "I saw Bryce, I guess you would call it his spirit—his physical body was still lying flat—I saw him just sit up, and he sort of stopped for a minute. Then he looked up and went through the ceiling tiles. He was happy and free of his shell."

"Why didn't you tell me?"

"We were fighting."

"You should have told me!"

"No, no, no, no. I was not getting in the middle of that one."

I was thinking, "This is so weird!"

"God needed to tell you," he continued. "I was not going to do anything to get between Bryce and his Momma. I told God, if He wants you to know Bryce is gone, He's going to have to be the one to tell you. You were not going to hear it from me, because I know you, and you would blame me for the rest of your life."

"Yeah, I probably would blame you," I instantly confessed. "Actually, I probably would."

And Jim said, "So he's ready."

"So where is he? Where do you think Bryce is?"

"I think he's with the Lord," Jim replied.

"But how could that be? His body is still alive. I don't understand."

"I don't understand either, maybe Bryce is still somehow attached to his body. He can't go into Heaven without his body dying. I don't see him up there. I don't see him watching. I saw him leave. I believe he's with Jesus. I think at this point it's medicine that's keeping him alive. Even if we brought him home, we would just be taking care of his physical body. Bryce isn't here anymore. Bryce is already gone."

"Well then, who have we been praying for?" I said, in agony. I was overwhelmed with the thoughts racing through my mind. Was he really gone? Was his body just a shell? Was he free?

Jim didn't have any answers either. He felt this unexpected vision was a gift, but he certainly didn't understand all of it.

It was all coming together. Jim had peace. Madison had peace. And I was getting peace. Before we hung up, Jim said again, "Well, don't sign any papers."

I said, "I know, I know. I won't."

Before the accident, Bryce left us with clear instructions as to what he would want us to do if something horrible ever happened to him, leaving him unable to live his life or care for himself. I could have turned off the machines in Japan, but I just couldn't imagine ever doing that. I fervently believed God would miraculously heal Bryce! I just knew He would! I now understand there are different ways of being healed.

When Bryce dies, it will always be beyond sad for us left behind, but Bryce's healing will be complete. He will simply take a last breath here with us, and his next breath will be in the presence of the Lord. He will be safe and sound with his Heavenly Father!

Chapter Twenty-Three

Comfort Care

Dr. Pai had offered to have a family meeting with us on Monday to answer any questions we had regarding options. But as it turned out, Jim, Madison, and I had already been able to reach a decision ourselves. It was time to stop fighting and to let go. It was now clear that Bryce had no true quality of life. We each had come to the same conclusion on our own and now again collectively as a family.

We knew we needed to follow Bryce's wishes.

Later that day, the director of the Polytrauma Program, Dr. Shane McNamee, unexpectedly poked his head into Bryce's room and asked how we were doing. I shared our family's discussions about Bryce's quality of life and how we had come to an agreement that we no longer wanted to artificially sustain his life.

"Oh, okay," he replied. "Come on down to my office." We literally walked right downstairs to his office and he started making things happen quickly.

He thought it would take a few days to get Bryce moved down to palliative care, which was normally the case. But when he called to get him accepted, they said they just happened to have a patient die and a room was now available. They made plans to move Bryce as soon as possible.

Dr. McNamee explained that we could change our mind at any time. But with our new decision, they thought it best to move

Bryce out of the unit as soon as possible. This was both for our sake and for the sake of the staff who had cared for him over these many months.

I was not expecting things to move this swiftly. But this did bring some comfort because it seemed like nothing went smoothly and swiftly in fighting to keep Bryce alive. But once our family agreed to allow Bryce to pass, it seemed like every door swung wide open for us. We couldn't help but feel this was the right thing and that God was blessing our decision.

I called Jim and told him what was discussed and that it was happening. "All right, Madi and I will come this weekend," he said. "Let me tell my boss and take care of things here, then we'll meet you in a few days."

We discussed the plans with Madison. Jim didn't want her to have to be present when Bryce was going through the dying process. They had discussed it already, and Madison did not want to remember her big brother in this way. She wanted to visit Bryce one last time to have the chance to say good-bye.

"I will bring her to Richmond to say good-bye," Jim explained. "I'll take her back to Monroe and get her situated with friends. Then I'll come back and stay through the end."

The medical staff came into Bryce's room and removed his stomach feeding tube. They left the end of the tube inside of him so they could give him the pain and comfort medications without giving him an actual shot with a needle.

They took out his IV and still left the little device in his arm to use for his comfort care. It was weird to see Bryce completely detached from everything after so many months. They stopped all fluids, except a little that was used to push his medications so they wouldn't get stuck. There would not be any more nutrition for Bryce.

I felt beyond sick about it. This was such a horrible situation. I never wanted to have to make this decision. As a person that struggles with my weight, I have issues with food. It has been a comfort to me for most of my life. Now, I was watching them remove food and water from my sweet Bryce. I was so sick knowing he would not be able to have another drink of water.

I felt panic that I couldn't comfort him. I had no idea if I could remain focused on Bryce's wishes and stay the course. This crossed all the lines of anything a mother would want for her child.

Sometimes a nurse would give Bryce a dose of his crushed or liquid medications, and it looked to me like they dumped in way too much water. Other nurses would give him just a tiny amount of water with his medications. I became obsessed with how much liquid they were introducing to his stomach, feeling angry that they were prolonging the dying process. I felt like such a terrible mother to even have these thoughts.

I just wanted his suffering to stop immediately, but in order for that to happen, Bryce would die. I hated having to be an active participant in Bryce's passing away process.

All of this got me to thinking about the last six months for Bryce. Since the accident he never had water brought to his lips or food brought to his mouth to be chewed and enjoyed. He had not had any of these comforts for a long time. Just thinking about this, I started wondering if he had been thirsty or starving this whole time and was unable to tell us. I thought about all the meals I ate sitting next to his bed because I didn't want to leave him. I wondered if deep inside he could smell all those meals I had eaten. I got very upset and asked a chaplain to pray with me about this.

After talking and praying with me, the chaplain asked a doctor to come and meet with me. The doctor told me that medically at the end of life the last thing a person wants is a drink or food. The doctor said it actually makes people feel sick. They have learned this from patients that are in the process of dying but awake and not in comas who can still speak with their loved ones and care providers.

You would think that they would want a good last meal, but that's not the way it is. Food and water are a comfort to me, and for a healthy person, but probably not to Bryce. That was good to hear because it goes against everything I would have thought.

Though we had made our decision to honor Bryce's wishes and let him go, I was still struggling. I knew now that it was absolutely impossible, outside of God's miraculous healing, for Bryce to ever have a good, conscious, quality life again. However, if we reconnected Bryce to a machine, would it show he still had brainwaves? Yes. Had his heart stopped beating? No.

But I also knew that he had suffered respiratory failure and went for an extended period of time with no, or far too little, oxygen. I understood that he couldn't swallow or digest. He would never be able to walk again. And he was blind.

The doctors tried everything they could think of to wake Bryce up and make him well. I tried everything I could think of to wake Bryce up and make him well.

I had begged God for a miracle. I was on my best behavior. Christian leaders had laid hands on him, anointed him with oil, and prayed the prayer of faith. I went to church and had whole congregations pray for him. We had over 13,000 prayer warriors on Facebook praying for him around the world. But he remained unchanged.

All of these thoughts were going through my mind. My gosh, what did we do? What have we put him through? He had so many procedures, surgeries, and pumps and tubes placed inside him. His wisdom teeth were removed, his eyes were checked, and he had daily therapies. We strapped him into exercise machines and made him stretch and work out, all while he was not even technically awake. He had multiple spinal taps. The ventilators, the tracheostomy, the scans, x-rays, MRIs, and all the rounds of blood work. This kid had been through the wringer for more than six months.

I felt bad for all he had been through on my watch, yet knew it was all done to try to help him come back to us.

I was doing everything I could to make things okay for the day Bryce woke up. The whole time I really believed that Bryce was going to be miraculously healed. But when I learned that his optic nerve had dissolved and that his brain was shrinking, it was like an internal switch turned off. "Enough! Enough! What kind of quality of life is this?"

This was an extremely hard thing to share. I felt like I was letting everyone down. I was actually thinking of turning off the Facebook page. But Madison was the one who said, "Mom, we need to tell Bryce's story. Don't stop now. People need to hear everything. You have been doing this every day. It's our journey, and it's okay."

We had already made the decision as a family, and his medical providers were in agreement with us, and we all knew privately what would be happening from here on out. We knew that we could change our mind at any time, if we wanted, but we were all in agreement and felt it was the right thing to do. We gave Bryce completely to God. It was up to God to heal him or take him home, at any time.

The psychologist was a Christian, and she said, "You're placing Bryce in God's hands. Do you understand? This is not you killing Bryce. You are saying, 'Okay God, here he is. If we aren't hearing from you, you have our permission to intervene.' Please, Holy Spirit, come and fix him, we've exhausted everything we know."

God works in threes, and we know He confirms things with his children. We felt like it was confirm, confirm, confirm. Jim saw something. Madison overheard and felt something. I heard something, and we all came together from three different places and are now in the exact same place.

The time had come to share our decision with the prayer warriors on Facebook. I needed to bring them up-to-date on what was going on, so they could continue to pray for Bryce—and for us.

I had posted on Facebook every single day since the accident, and I had tried desperately to hold on to my hope and faith that Bryce would be healed. So when we started talking about letting Bryce go, I didn't even know how to say publicly what I wanted to say anymore. I wanted to make sure that I didn't lie, but I wasn't sure how much I would, or should, share. It was important to me that I not mince words, or embellish, or skirt around the issues. So I asked the director and the psychiatrist at the Polytrauma Unit to help me write this vital post.

Facebook Update: Tuesday 4/16/13

Bryce's condition, with multiple layers of catastrophic brain injuries, has continued to pull him farther away from us. We recently received additional difficult information, and unfortunately, we realize we can no longer sustain his precious and young life.

His amazing doctors and medical team have shown such kindness and care. They have literally exhausted every possible idea they could think of to help him beat this and somehow come back to us. I will always be grateful to them.

Our family has decided to honor Bryce's written wishes, allowing him to pass naturally and peacefully. I can tell you, as his Momma, it is much harder to put his wishes ahead of mine, which is perhaps why I haven't even allowed myself to consider these wishes prior to this point. I had to try everything first.

With all this said, my trust remains solid in the Lord. I trust Him to heal Bryce, like I have always confessed. This healing is the ultimate healing. How could I not be grateful that with his last breath here with me, his next will be in the presence of the Lord?

I have shared our family's journey with you the last six-plus months, and honestly, I thought long and hard about just closing down this Facebook Prayer Page because I don't have the strength to battle everyone's questions, ideas, different beliefs, and possible judgment calls.

My sweet daughter, on the other hand, is the braver one. She insisted that I "finish our story." I decided she is right. You have all been so faithful to us throughout this journey, and I know in my heart you will continue to love and pray for us during this horrible time.

Jim, Madison, and I are thankful we have a future with Bryce, and eventually we will be okay.

Psalm 46:1 (NLT)
"God is our refuge and strength, always ready to help in times of trouble."

Psalm 56:8 (NLT)
"You keep track of all my sorrows. You have collected all my tears in your bottle. You have recorded each one in your book."

Specific prayer request:

For us to have an extra dose of grace, mercy, and strength

Love, Cathy

Chapter Twenty-Four

No Papers to Sign

Jim had told me from the very beginning not to sign any papers. He wanted to take that burden upon himself, to shelter me. He didn't want me to have to live with that. But as it turned out, we never had to sign any papers when moving Bryce to palliative care. So God blessed both Jim and me in this area.

I had even asked where the papers were and when we needed to sign them. "There are no papers," Dr. Pai explained. "We've exhausted everything medically that we can do for him. Bryce is now succumbing to his injuries from the accident."

Facebook Update: Tuesday 4/16/13

Today was an extremely tough day. We had to move Bryce out of the Polytrauma Unit on the second floor down to the Palliative Care Unit on the first floor.

We would have loved to keep Bryce upstairs, surrounded by all the familiar and caring medical professionals who have become family to us. This could not happen though because it would not be fair to the many heroes that have taken such great care of Bryce all these months, trying their best to help him heal, wake up, and become strong once again. We cannot expect them to now watch Bryce slowly pass away.

The Polytrauma Unit staff did have a big meeting with the Emerging Consciousness Program director. Every shift, day and night, had a similar meeting regarding Bryce. We were comforted to hear every single employee involved in Bryce's care during his stay fully respected our family's decision to finally stop. Not one person raised their hand when asked if anyone disagreed or had any issue whatsoever with our decision.

We were all in agreement.

While all of Bryce's belongings were being packed up to be moved, each of the Polytrauma staff came in to his hospital room, one at a time, to say their good-byes, offer their support, and give us hugs, kisses, and prayers. There were a whole lot of tears, and then we headed downstairs to begin palliative care in "Journey's Way."

Life Offline

At the end of his life, I was scared to death of Bryce. Not Bryce my son, but the pieces of Bryce that were left inside his severely brain-injured body. I felt so horrible for feeling this way, but I was more than afraid. I was absolutely terrified by the scary moaning and stiffness. It became more and more clear that Bryce was gone, and only a shell of a body remained.

Yet despite my fears, I wanted to be close to my baby as we were saying good-bye. So at my request, the palliative care nurse helped me get into Bryce's bed with him. We moved him from the center of the bed over to the side, and then I got in on the other side. The nurse pulled up and locked the metal side handrail, and then she went out and closed the door behind her so I could have some privacy and hold Bryce.

When I reached my arm around Bryce to hug him, he let out a moan, perhaps because of the stimulation, and his back arched. Any stimulation can cause a storm, and I guess that's what happened. He made a horrible noise, like a growl.

I completely went into a panic and tried to get myself out of the bed. But the nurse had lifted the rail, and I couldn't get out. I tried for a few more seconds but couldn't get the side rail to release. At this point, I just started screaming for help. The nurse opened the door and quickly got me out of the bed. I don't think I have ever been so scared. I actually had envisioned Bryce trying to bite me if he could.

Madison and I talked later. and she had the same fearful feeling, as if it weren't Bryce in there anymore.

I was heartbroken that I couldn't hold Bryce and love on him. I just wanted one last special moment of connection with my child, to comfort him somehow and to have that loving moment to remember for the rest of my life.

This sounds crazy, but in my mind Bryce seemed like a zombie. I hated myself for being fearful of my own sweet son. I was so ashamed. I was heartbroken for everything that had happened and that Bryce's life was going to end like this.

I cried all day and I begged God to forgive me for being afraid. I was riddled with guilt for being afraid of my helpless son in a vegetative, comatose state. I begged God to quickly bring Bryce home.

Although the setting in the Palliative Care Unit is one of peace, I was beyond terrified. I was so upset about Bryce, and I was panicking about whether or not we were making the right decision.

I was afraid that God was mad at us, thinking we are murdering Bryce. I had been crying out to God, telling Him I love Bryce more than anything, and asking Him to still heal him, even in this midnight hour!

I kept repenting over and over again, asking God to take me with Bryce—or even better, to take me instead of him. I was plagued with fear. I had images in my head of screaming at the top of my lungs for the nurses to once again plug in all of the medical tubing.

As my anxiety level continued to steeply climb, the Polytrauma Patient and Family Education Coordinator, Barbara Bauserman, came down to see how Bryce and I were doing. Barbara had become one of my dearest friends and confidants over the last several months. As soon as she entered the room, I told her I was so scared and felt extremely sick.

"It would be easier to just bring Bryce home," I cried, "and take care of him in our living room for the rest of his life. I have no other plans other than loving and taking care of Madison and Bryce. They are my life."

"All I ever wanted was to be their Momma," I explained. "Now, here I am doing something so horrible." I paused and wiped my tears. "Yet I also know that I'm doing what Bryce would have wanted."

As I finished, I watched her close her eyes and take a deep breath. Then she calmly and simply asked, "Cathy, what is it you're afraid of?"

"I'm afraid Bryce is going to wake up, and sit straight up in his bed, and it would be too late to help him. Then it would be my fault for letting him die."

Again, very calmly and with a beautiful smile she said, "Cathy, if Bryce sits up, we will praise God, put an IV in him, and bring him back upstairs."

Her words brought instant comfort and clarity. I had been so panicked with all of the horrible emotions and guilt, I had completely forgotten that we had placed Bryce in God's hands.

I knew beyond a doubt that if God wanted to heal Bryce, He could do it easily! The God we serve brought people back to life in the Bible, so bringing Bryce to the Palliative Care Unit was not taking Bryce out of God's reach.

Barbara explained that the word "palliate" means "to remove suffering." That's what we wanted to do for our son. I had begged God to help me stop the suffering for Bryce. Once I thought about this for a moment, the fear that had been choking me all day long disappeared. The calm and peace of God once again washed over me.

We continued to have visitors from the Polytrauma Unit staff all the way until the end. The doctors, nurses, therapists, and even other patients' families that we had become close with over the last few months were coming down to check on us, which was very comforting.

Bryce's palliative care nurse gave him a shot of medication to dry up his secretions so he didn't feel like he was drowning. Most people have what is called a "death rattle" in their throats and chests as they approach the end of life. This medication helped to clear some of that up.

My 21-year-old son was literally dying in slow motion in front of my eyes. Nothing about this was normal, easy, or felt okay, yet it was all part of the process. I could feel the separation happening.

I would still see the other mothers or family members at the hospital or the Fisher House and I couldn't help but wonder why their loved one woke up and Bryce didn't. Were they better than us? Were they more deserving? Was God mad at us? Was he mad at Bryce? I couldn't help thinking these thoughts, and it was a very confusing time.

I felt bad thinking these things because many of us had spent so much time together and had gotten to know each other at the Fisher House and the hospital in these last few months. I knew that many of them really cared about Bryce and our family. We had cried together, been mad together, had happy moments together, and were real with each other. I trusted many of them with my thoughts and feelings, and they had also trusted me with theirs. But it still hurt that their children were recovering and mine was dying.

Bryce's room in the Palliative Care Unit had a sidewalk right outside, so I could see people coming in and out of the hospital. I closed the curtains because there was just too much life outside. I also kept the lights down. I turned on nice soft music and kept everything quiet to keep Bryce as free from stimulation as possible. I didn't want him to have any storms or seizures. I just wanted him to close his eyes and peacefully die.

That was what I was hoping for. This was no longer a recovery. This was the dying process. He had to die one minute at a time, and they said it could take up to four weeks. That would have been normal for someone Bryce's age with a healthy body. We now knew the brain wasn't working. So without constant medical aid, his body would soon stop working too.

At this point Bryce was curled up, bent out of proportion, blind, with his fingers tightly clenched His body had its own set of problems, but his organs were still healthy. And so we watched … and waited.

Facebook Update: Thursday 4/18/13

I apologize for not posting an update last night. I will do my best to try and send out a little something when I can. It won't be every day though.

I'm enjoying every second I can with my brave, sweet son. He is so peaceful and beautiful. I will cherish these precious moments forever. The Lord's magnificent, loving presence is here with us.

Thank you, Father for your many blessings and your wonderful sweetness, even in the sting.

Our family appreciates all of your kind words of support, your love, and your faithful and heartfelt prayers! We know only God could provide the thousands of prayer warriors who remain by our side.

In time, I will be able to invite you to join us as we celebrate Bryce's new life and mourn his early departure. We will have a funeral in Monroe, North Carolina, a military memorial service at Langley Air Force Base, in Hampton, Virginia, and he will be laid to rest, with full honors, at Arlington National Cemetery in Virginia.

Bryce loved Arlington Cemetery!

I tried to figure out exactly why Arlington was so important to me. Then I remembered the time I went with Bryce to Arlington in his junior year of high school. We walked together through the Robert E. Lee House. We looked at the engraving on many of the headstones. Then we watched the somber pageantry of the changing of the guard at the Tomb of the Unknown Soldier.

Bryce kept saying things like, "Momma, look at this. Isn't this sad?" and "Look at this one. Wow." We walked around the manicured grounds for an entire day. Before this, Bryce had a fear of cemeteries. He had been playing tag in a cemetery as a child when he slipped and fell into a hole next to a gravestone, all the way up to his waist. It freaked him out for years. But after we traveled to Arlington, he changed his mind. He told me, "If I ever die in the military, I want to be buried in Arlington."

I met with the military casualty liaisons and also with a representative of the funeral home assigned to take care of Bryce's remains. This was one of the most difficult things I've ever had to do, and yet it had to be done. I had to make all the preparations before he had even passed. Jim was still at home, so alone, I picked out a casket. I also had to make decisions about his funeral and military memorial service.

They explained the many options, and then we paired Bryce's wishes with mine. On the inside, my heart was breaking, but on the outside, I was responding, "Oh I love this casket, Bryce would love this one."

I asked if Bryce could be buried in his jeans and favorite lucky green T-shirt. The liaison kindly, but professionally, shared that most active duty troops are proudly buried in their dress blues. I caught the clue and quickly moved forward with their great idea. After all, nothing but the best for my boy!

The military liaisons assured me Bryce would have all of his earned ribbons sewn onto his uniform, and his extra Senior Airman stripe, earned on Christmas Eve, would also be displayed. I requested an open casket visitation so all of his friends back in our hometown would have a chance to say their final good-byes as well.

Jim and Madison arrived in Richmond on Friday, April 19, for the first time since Bryce had been moved to palliative care. They would be here for the weekend, and then Jim planned to drive Madison home.

To add insult to great injury, Jim told me he lost his job the previous day. The VA social worker had given Jim the Family Medical Leave Act (FMLA) forms to give to his employer, so he could take time off work to be with me and Bryce as he passes.

Eager to spend the last days of Bryce's precious life with his son, Jim went to work and requested the forms be signed. His employer replied, "We don't know what FMLA is, and we don't do that here." In brief, after a few more uncomfortable minutes meeting with three separate people up the company chain, Jim was officially "let go." Right there on the spot, he had to turn in his tools and his company truck. Then they ordered a coworker to drive him the hour-and-twenty-minutes to our home.

Talk about kicking a man when he's down! He was fired for requesting time off to be with his son as he passed away. It was unbelievable!

When he gave me the news, I shot back, ",What do you mean you lost your job? Have you given them the FMLA paperwork?"

"Yes, I gave them the forms."

"Well then, they have to give it to you. It's part of the Family Medical Leave Act."

"No, they said they don't do it."

"Yes, they have to do it—it's federal."

"No, they don't have it where I work."

I kept asking, frantically, "Did you tell them that Bryce is dying?"

We were both getting very upset and angry.

I could have said, "Oh honey, I'm sorry. At least we are together, and we're okay. We can get though anything." Instead, I freaked out. Putting things in perspective, Jim losing his job was not as serious as Bryce's condition, which was close to death. I still overreacted, panicking and crying about a job loss instead of the pain of what was happening to our son. I had to hold it together when it came to Bryce, but everything else was off the table. I was an emotional ticking time bomb. A simple thing like a missing coffee cup sent me over the edge.

I wanted to call his employers and tell them off. Jim, on the other hand, seemed to be okay about it. "It's just a job." Honestly, he did add in a few colorful words. But at that moment we needed to be fully present, and calm, for Bryce.

On Saturday, some of our family and close friends came to the hospital to spend a little time with Bryce. We all knew this would most likely be the last chance they would have to tell Bryce their final good-byes. So we made no official plans and just let the day unfold as it happened.

Later in the evening, Jim, Madison, and I all left the hospital for a couple of hours in search of nice suits and dresses for Bryce's funeral. This felt all wrong, since he was still alive, but it was something that had to be done.

We each wanted to pick out something nice, something that would make Bryce proud. Just in case God allowed Bryce to see us, we wanted him to know his Dad, Mom, and sister all dressed up nicely for him. Jim found two nice suits and I found a dress with a jacket and a pant suit. We were unable to find something nice for Madison to wear.

When we returned to Bryce's room, I turned on the CD player next to his bed. As the music played quietly in the background, I told Jim and Madison about the two new handmade, and very heartfelt, music CDs Bryce received from Dr. Pai and Michael Dardozzi. They had each created and delivered Bryce a personal music CD full of songs they felt would comfort him on his journey home.

It was the perfect gift for Bryce! Neither of them knew the other was also creating one. They both understood and appreciated the profound affect music had in Bryce's life, and so with that in mind, on their own time, they each created a going home themed music CD to bless Bryce. Two special gifts I will treasure forever.

Our family weekend was coming to a close, and it was time for Jim to take Madison home. She would be staying with the family of one of her best friends from school. We had discussed Madison staying in the hospital with us, but as a family we decided it would be best for Madison to say her good-byes to her big brother now, while he appears to be sleeping peacefully.

Madison was adamant that she did not want to remember Bryce in his final moments. She knew he would be with Jesus, and she said she would faithfully continue to hold on to that belief. She had been working hard to stay focused at school since the accident happened, and so she wanted to go home to stay on track with her grades. Jim also thought it would be best for her to go back to school and keep moving forward.

I was the only one who kept asking Madison "Are you sure? You will never get another chance to be with Bryce after he passes." I just didn't know what the right thing to do or say as a parent in this situation. So I prayed and asked God for His wisdom to do and say what is right—and then also for mercy to cover us in case I ended up doing it all wrong.

I did think it was a good idea to allow Madison a say in these decisions. She has a good head on her shoulders and a compassionate heart, and I trusted her judgment to help set the boundaries she was comfortable with. None of us had been through anything like this before, and we were all doing our best.

This would be the last time Madison would see Bryce alive. I knew it would be an extremely difficult time for her.

When it was time for Madison to say good-bye, she asked if she could be alone with him for a minute. She later told me that she said, "Bye, Bryce." Then she gave him a kiss on the cheek and said, "I love you."

After Jim and Madison left, I settled in next to Bryce, continuing to pray for help, completely exhausted in every way.

All of this, every single moment of it, was gut-wrenching pain from where I sat. I was reminded once again that I couldn't protect my two beautiful children from this terrible reality. Oh how I wished I could turn back the clock and both kids could be little again!

Realizing time was short, as soon as they made it back to Monroe, Jim took Madison shopping for a special dress and makeup. I hadn't asked him to do any of this for Madison.

Jim explained to the ladies behind the counter that Madison's brother was dying, and she needed something nice to wear to his funeral. They immediately flew into action, trying on makeup and teaching her how to apply it properly. They gathered some outfits for her to consider. Jim bought her some high-quality makeup and two separate outfits, a black dress and a navy blue dress, so she had a choice of things to wear. I was so blessed that Jim created this special moment for Madison in the midst of a very difficult time.

Chapter Twenty-Five

Renewing Our Vows

When Jim returned from taking Madison home, the hospital social worker, Keneshia, came down to see us. She walked in the room and started to say, "Hey Jim..."

Before she could continue, I blurted out, "They fired him."

She seemed shocked. "What do mean?"

Jim explained what had happened with his employer when he gave them the FMLA forms and said that he was told that they don't do the Family Medical Leave Act.

Keneshia shook her head. "No, no, no. This is a federal program. They can't, 'not do it.' Let's go to my office." Jim left with her to get new forms and to get the situation straightened out.

After they left the Palliative Care Unit, I called Jim's employee union, the International Brotherhood of Electrical Workers (IBEW), to complain about what had happened. It just so happened that the lady who answered the phone in the IBEW office had been following my Facebook prayer page for Bryce for the last few months. We had not known this. Because she was aware of Bryce's situation, she had extra mercy on us when I told her that Jim was let go for asking if he could take off under FMLA.

She took personal offense over the entire situation. "Oh, no, no, no! Could you hold on for a minute?"

A few minutes later, she came back on my phone and told me she had spoken with Jim's employer, educated him about FMLA, and that everything had been worked out. It was that quick, and Jim had his job back! I thanked her for all of her help. She told me she would continue to pray for all of us.

When Jim and the social worker returned, he told me he had received a call on his cell phone from his boss in Charlotte. They told him he can have his "@*x#!-ing" job back so long as he was back within the 12-week time period.

There had been no mention of Bryce or any well wishes for Jim and his family. It was just strictly a business deal. Jim was a great employee and had worked extremely hard for years with that company. I often wondered if his employer even realized how much their lack of care and support for Jim hurt our family. This was not a guy asking to take a vacation. His only son was dying. He simply wanted an opportunity to be with him as he passed.

On the flip side, Jim also said that this was not a personal thing. This is just normal life in the construction world. At the end of the day, getting his job back was a victory.

Jim had to drive all the way back to Charlotte to turn in new paperwork with a doctor's signature and get it officially approved by his employer.

I don't think we will ever forget their lack of care and compassion for two men who proudly served their country. They didn't care about Jim or Bryce.

Jim made it safely back to Richmond and stayed with me and Bryce for the duration of his time in palliative care. Jim didn't get to be a part of planning the funeral or picking the casket, so we went over everything again with him to make sure we didn't miss any details. I wanted Jim to have a say in all that.

Friends and family continued to stop in and say good-bye to Bryce. Many offered prayers for divine healing, absolute peace, and God's perfect will to be accomplished in Bryce's life.

Gwyn asked if her family could come up to spend time with us and see Bryce. Their son, Aaron, grew up with Bryce and considered him a best friend. He had read my Facebook post when I said we were no longer able to sustain Bryce, and he thought Bryce was already dead. Aaron had called Gwyn crying so hysterically, she didn't even recognize it was her son. When they realized Bryce was still alive in palliative care, they all wanted to come to say their good-byes.

I asked Jim first if it would be okay, and he said yes.

When they came to visit us in palliative care, they went in to see Bryce for a short visit, but then they stayed with us for the entire day. Aaron's wife was going to have a baby in the next couple of months, and they were excited to tell me that they decided they would add Bryce as a second middle name. Everyone was so excited, a new baby on the way! It was going to be GREAT for them.

But things were horrible for us, and, once again, I was feeling jealous of their good news. I acted polite and excited, but again this was just too much. Life for us was ending, while theirs was expectant with new beginnings. It was bittersweet. We loved Aaron, and I knew Bryce would have been happy for him. I still felt torn and wanted to be appreciative and social, but I also just wanted to be with my son.

Everyone was getting hungry, and people were asking, "Who wants wings? Who wants pizza?" It was like a family reunion, and Bryce was lying in the other room dying.

I had all these horrible things going through my mind, and this was clearly not a good time to be having a party just outside of Bryce's hospital room. This was why we limited visitors in the first place. But I had to force myself to be gracious until I could get back to Bryce's bedside, which is where I wanted to be all along.

Bryce initially had a horrible time in palliative care. It was not a peaceful thing where he just lay in bed and didn't move. He ended up having a negative reaction to the morphine, which caused him to make very loud audible moans almost like a growling sound. It was actually frightening.

Bryce had been on a regimen of 28 different drugs while he was in the Polytrauma Unit. So when he moved to the Palliative Care Unit, they discontinued most of his medications, except for the ones bringing him comfort. His body had to come off all those drugs pretty much cold turkey.

They decided to give him morphine to bring his body comfort. It didn't seem to work, so they doubled the dosage. Again, it didn't work, so they tripled it. Now instead of bringing comfort care, the morphine was having the exact opposite effect. I was so upset about this. The twisting, moaning, and growling went on for a few days, getting worse and worse. Finally, I ran hysterically down to the chapel, begging God to help Bryce. I wanted so desperately for Bryce to be free and safe in Jesus' arms. Watching my son continue to be plagued with this pain—whether or not he comprehended it—and not being able to comfort him, was tormenting me.

The doctors met us in the chapel and discussed Bryce's condition. Suddenly the palliative care doctor said, "You know what? Maybe it's his medicine. Let's switch back to the fentanyl that he had upstairs and see if that helps."

This worked immediately. After his first dose, he stopped all moaning and seemed to finally be at peace.

As Bryce's physical body continues to fail I'm wondering if he can see us with his spiritual eyes. In the book *Heaven Is For Real*, as the little boy was dying, he found himself out of and above his body with the ability to see and hear his family and medical attendants around him. Just in case Bryce is experiencing that reality, every once in a while I look above Bryce's body and talk to him as if I can see him without any injuries at all.

"Bryce, I know your body suffered a severe brain injury, but your spirit is still perfectly fine." Then I smile and tell him how much I love him, how proud I am to be his Momma, and how much I'm going to miss him.

I even told him I'm jealous he gets to go to Heaven and see Jesus before me. If he is able to see and hear everything around him in the spirit, I think he loves the music and visitors that have been surrounding him.

Our Polytrauma family has been coming down around the clock, checking on all three of us. We can clearly see Bryce has touched each of these amazing medical professionals. Many have broken down in tears as they share that they would be making the same choice we are -- letting us know they "get it" and their hearts are breaking right along with ours.

Many have also shared how they have been changed in a positive way while taking care of Bryce and watching our family love and support him throughout this journey.

Life Offline

Bryce's doctor estimated it could take up to two more weeks before he passed. We had to wait for Bryce's physical body to catch up to the high level of deterioration that has already occurred throughout his brain. Every part of my being ached for Bryce. What parent can just sit and watch their child slowly die?

I cried out to God through my anguish. "Oh God, please help Bryce. Heal him or take him home with you. Please don't leave him here broken, unfixable, with any more pain and suffering."

I felt so bad that there was no quick way through this for Bryce. Then I would immediately hate myself for even thinking about the possibility of a quick way for Bryce to die. It was pure hell. I was sad and confused, and I still didn't even know for sure if God was going to be mad at me for stopping the life-sustaining treatments. I never thought this would happen to my child. I couldn't believe this is happening to Bryce.

At 5 p.m., Jim said, "Let's get out of here for a little while, get dinner and a coffee, and then we'll come back in a bit." At first I refused because I didn't want Bryce to be alone. I was worried he might pass away alone while we were gone.

Jim reminded me of what the doctor had said earlier, that he most likely had two weeks left to live. "We need to get out of this place. Nothing is going to happen tonight."

Jim was insistent on going, so I decided to go with him. We drove around for a while, then decided to go to a local mall I had been to once before. There was a restaurant there that I knew was good. Once inside, we sat on opposite sides of the table and barely spoke to each other. Our marriage was in so much trouble at this point, we weren't even fighting anymore, just existing as a couple until this was over.

After dinner was eaten, and coffee was served, Jim looked straight into my eyes, and said in an extremely serious tone, "So are we doing this?"

I asked what he meant.

"Are we done? Is the marriage over?"

"Yeah, I guess so."

"All right!" he said, while nodding his head in agreement.

We continued to sit in silence, sipping our coffee. After a couple minutes, I said, "You know what's sad? If I ever get remarried…"

At this point he cut me off mid-sentence, and said, "Oh hell, no! I will never remarry! I've had enough!"

"Anyway", I continued, "if I ever get remarried, I hope I find someone just like you. Seriously, I love you. Your strengths are my weaknesses, and my strengths are your weaknesses. We are perfect for each other. But we're both so strong and bullheaded at times; we just really need God to help us!"

As the evening progressed and another cup of coffee was poured, we began to talk and heal. We were able to trust each other with our hurts and scars, and God blessed us by instantaneously healing our broken hearts—and our broken marriage.

We made new vows to each other that night that there would be no more talk of divorce. We would simply keep going through the good times and the bad times, and, with God's help, we will make it!

As we walked out of the restaurant, we noticed a jewelry store a couple doors away. Immediately I was reminded that when I started this journey, leaving for Japan to be with Bryce, I was in a left arm cast and unable to wear my wedding ring due to excessive swelling. As crazy as it sounds, Jim was also in a left-handed cast, unable to wear his wedding ring either. Eventually our wrists had healed, our casts had come off, and yet neither of us ever put our wedding rings back on.

After talking to Jim about it, we decided to walk into the jewelry store and look for new rings to go with our new vows. Together, we picked a new bridal set.

We came back to the hospital and I told Bryce what happened. "Don't worry, we renewed our vows to each other tonight. We just bought new rings. We are going to stay married.

"It's sad for us that you will be leaving, but I am so happy you will be with Jesus. We're going to take good care of Madison. You don't need to worry about any of us.

"Now this is very important, Bryce. You need to keep a watch out for Jesus. You will be going to heaven soon, and I'm so excited for you. Don't be scared, and do not go with anyone else."

Jim was standing on one side of the bed holding Bryce's hand, and I was on the other side, holding the other hand. As tears streamed down my cheeks I told my only son, "It's okay for you to go. We will all be okay. We will miss you, and we love you very much."

As soon as I finished talking to Bryce, Jim seemed to sense something. All of a sudden he jerked his head around and looked up near the ceiling in the left back corner of Bryce's room. I looked where he seemed to be looking and saw nothing. When Jim turned back around toward me he had a very strange, wide-eyed look on his face. It immediately caught my attention and I felt instant goose bumps all over me.

Once again, Jim quickly turned his head around. This time it was to the other corner, the left front corner of Bryce's room, and then back over to the left back corner. He was scanning his eyes back and forth on that side of the hospital room, looking up near the ceiling. I was staring wide-eyed, watching Jim and wondering what was happening. I wanted to see whatever it was that he was seeing, but again I saw nothing.

When Jim turned his head back toward me a second time, I looked at him and in an urgent almost whisper said, "What? What do you see?"

Calmly he said, "He's getting ready to go."

I felt a jolt of pain go through me. "No!" I began arguing with Jim. "The doctor said he has two more weeks!"

Jim looked directly in to my eyes and said, "He is getting ready to go soon."

Now I believed his words. He had been right about these kinds of things too many times before. "Is he leaving tonight?"

A few seconds later Jim calmly and authoritatively said, "No, Bryce is passing tomorrow."

Chapter Twenty-Six

7,777 Days on Earth

I stayed awake the entire night in Bryce's room. After Jim had his vision he said, "We're not going anywhere." I was afraid from that point on to even use the restroom or leave the room for any reason. We lay down on the sofa bed and Jim fell asleep, but I just couldn't.

I just couldn't take my eyes off Bryce. I didn't want him to die alone. I was listening for his breathing. I kept looking and listening because he didn't have a heart monitor.

The staff had given us a pamphlet on dying that said his kidneys might flush out right before he dies, or he might want to eat something, or he might get a burst of energy. The problem was that this list was for a normal patient, not a brain-damaged person like Bryce. I reviewed the list and thought, "Wow, he might wake up and feel really alive before he dies." So I stayed awake all night to see if any of these things were going to happen.

Jim woke up around 7 a.m. and we folded the sofa bed away. I still wouldn't go to the bathroom, because the hospice nurse had told me that in her experience, as soon as a family member leaves the room, even for a minute to use the bathroom, that's when a lot of patients pass away. I didn't want that to happen. I wanted to be with him when he left.

As the day went on, Bryce's breathing just got worse and worse. The death rattle started in the afternoon, right after lunch. For the first time, I felt like I could hear Bryce's voice in his coughing. It reminded me of the old Bryce. The nurse came in and gave him some medicine to dry him up after a while because it sounded like he was choking.

Then around two o'clock, the breathing changed again. It was out of rhythm. It was the kind of breathing where you breathe, then stop breathing. Then breathe, and then stop breathing. We had been told that this kind of breathing takes place at the end of life.

"What do you think?" I asked Jim.

"It's coming," he answered. "It is near. It won't be long now."

That's when we closed the door to our room, so we could have privacy. In the Palliative Care Unit, when you close your door, the nurses respect your alone time. They won't bother you until you open it.

We were watching him very closely, and then we noticed another change. Suddenly red splotchy coloring started popping up all over the place. It looked like a case of measles gone wild.

"It's time," Jim said calmly.

Suddenly supernatural strength welled up inside of me, and I was literally delivering Bryce to Jesus. There was no anxiety at all. It was the grace of God. I was holding his right hand, and Jim was holding his left.

"Your body might be broken," I declared loudly, "your brain might be broken, but nothing is wrong with your spirit. You know who Jesus is. You go look for him now. You are getting ready to die, Bryce. It's almost time. Don't be scared. You go look for Jesus and don't stop anywhere, and don't talk to anyone else."

At the same time, I was asking the Lord to accept Bryce. I was reciting Scripture and reminding Bryce that Jesus died on the cross for his sins.

As I was saying all of this, I looked over at Jim, and he was just beaming. I could tell he was proud of me. I just kept telling Bryce that we were going to be fine, that we loved him, and that we'd see him again soon with Jesus.

It was my last chance to tell Bryce everything that was in my heart. Later, I told Madison that I realized at that moment, the only reason I even had kids was to teach them about Jesus. I wasted so much of my life doing my own thing, raising the kids, making mac and cheese, and putting on movies. But when your child is getting ready to die right in front of you, you suddenly take a really good look at what you've done in your life.

I told Madison that all I was supposed to do with her and Bryce was to teach them about Jesus, live my life for Jesus, and tell the world about Jesus. As lazy Christians at times, we are all living for ourselves, on our own, and that is wrong. I told her we still have to live our lives, but not to make the same mistakes I had made, forgetting the purpose of why we are even here on this earth.

I hoped I hadn't blown it with Bryce. When I looked at all the evidence, I came to the conclusion that he is now with Jesus. I just have to have faith and believe it.

When we first arrived in the Palliative Care Unit, it hit me that Bryce was going to be gone soon. As we go through our days, we are not really thinking these things all the way through. But while we were waiting for him to die, we started realizing, THIS IS IT!

Suddenly, Bryce stopped breathing for a stretch, and Jim and I looked at each other. Then he started back up for a while. Then he stopped for another stretch. And then, once again, he started breathing again. This happened a few times, and then Jim said, "It's going to be very soon now."

Madison asked me to promise her to call her when he was dying. We wanted her to be able to say good-bye to Bryce before he died, so we called her on the cell phone.

Madison was with her friends, Kaitlin and Karleigh. Their prom was happening in less than twenty-four hours, so they were trying various beauty tricks to make their skin look nice. They had just finished mixing together olive oil and coffee grounds. The girls had just smeared the concoction on their faces and were howling with laughter when the phone rang.

Madison picked up the phone, and it was Jim letting her know that Bryce was dying and she needed to say good-bye. She immediately ran down the hall and went into the bathroom to be alone.

"I love you, Bryce," Madison said through her tears. "You've been a good brother. I will see you again soon in heaven."

Suddenly Bryce stopped breathing, and his skin instantly went from red and splotchy to white. Jim picked up the phone and said to Madison, "Okay, we'll call you back."

Madison didn't know it then, but as she was talking to him, Bryce breathed his final breath. Madison went back into the bedroom and lay down crying. Her two friends lay down on either side of her and joined her in weeping.

I wondered if Bryce would start breathing again as he had before. Jim lowered his ear down on his chest and listened. He heard his heart beat and then there was silence. Jim lifted his head and said, "No, he's gone. I just heard his final heartbeat."

I didn't know if he was above us, watching us like in the movies, so I looked up toward the ceiling and I told him good-bye and said that we loved him. I wondered if Jesus was there in the room with us or if there were angels. A lot of thoughts were racing through my mind.

Suddenly time stopped; the world stopped; the universe stopped. It was just nothingness. It was an abrupt end. It was the cold stare, and then, "Now what?"

Then I remember the chaplain coming in. It could have been ten seconds or ten minutes later, I don't know. He said he was sorry for our loss and prayed a prayer of benediction. He asked us if we needed anything else and we said, "No, but thank you." Then he left as quickly as he had arrived.

We were in shock.

His death was not peaceful. I thought if you're a Christian, you have a peaceful death. Some of the hospice ladies told us stories about patients lifting their hands in the air before they passed. Some patients said things like, "I can see heaven." I was hoping for something like that to happen with Bryce, but I was completely forgetting that he wasn't even conscious.

After Bryce passed, Jim wanted something special that would always be Bryce. Similar to a baby's footprint being recorded at birth, Jim took a photo of Bryce's thumbprint, capturing his unique identity forever. Jim thought maybe someday we could turn this into a piece of jewelry, or a dog tag. It would be a one of a kind. It would be Bryce.

Dr. Pai typically parked in employee parking, on the other side of the hospital, but all of those parking spots were full that day, so he had to park near the Palliative Care Unit area. As he was leaving for the day, he remembered that Bryce still had the baclofen pump inside of his abdomen. This device had an alarm in it, to alert when it needed to be refilled. Dr. Pai wanted to turn it off so that this alarm would not go off at Bryce's funeral and scare everyone to death. He decided to go back to his office to get the key to turn it off.

He got out of his car and walked right into the Palliative Care Unit, not knowing that Bryce had died. So when Jim opened the door, Dr. Pai was standing right there. He wasn't expecting Bryce to pass for two more weeks. It was a Friday, and he would have been gone for the weekend. He came in the room and I got to hug him before I hugged anyone else. I went from holding Bryce's hand to hugging and crying with Dr. Pai. It was so amazing.

Dr. Pai teared up a little bit because it affected him. "You guys have been through so much," he said somberly. He called the attending doctor and they both checked Bryce's vitals. She looked at the clock and then checked with her stethoscope for a heartbeat. Then she called it.

Bryce Powers died at 4:40 p.m. on Friday, April 26, 2013.

Dr. Pai asked if we wanted an autopsy performed. We had initially said no until we were told that allowing a thorough autopsy on Bryce could help other brain-injured patients. From the findings, doctors would be able to learn a lot about the numerous effects of the multiple layers of brain injuries he suffered. There was still so much to learn about the brain and brain injuries. We agreed to the autopsy with the understanding that it could help other patients and families like ours.

We asked if there was any chance of organ donation because Bryce was a very big advocate. Even in high school, he did a project trying to get others to sign up to be donors. After making the decision to allow Bryce to succumb to his injuries, we hoped to at least let Bryce be a donor to save other lives with his organs.

We were informed that sadly, none of his organs could be donated. They all had to die with Bryce. Because he was in a vegetative state and wasn't officially "brain dead" on a ventilator, they couldn't give him anesthesia and harvest his organs. It would have been against the law to remove his organs from his body. His perfect heart, liver, lungs, and everything else they would normally donate, also had to die a slow death, which destroyed them. In the end nothing could be saved or shared.

Dr. Pai called upstairs to let the staff in 2B know, and the psychiatrist, psychologist, and several nurses came down to say good-bye and give us a hug.

After everyone left the room and we were alone with Bryce's body, I had that same horrible feeling as I did when I received the very first phone call. I didn't know what to do with myself. I walked over to the cupboard, which was full of Bryce's things and wondered what we were going to take. I started blindly walking around the room with that familiar feeling of panic.

I didn't know what to do or where to start. And Jim said, "No, no, you go back to the Fisher House and do what you need to do. I'll pack up."

I started arguing with him. "No, you don't know where everything goes."

So he grabbed my shoulders, just like he did the morning we received the first phone call. He put his face in my face, made me look at him in his eyes, and said, "I've got this. I will pack up the room. You can leave and go on over to the Fisher House."

I was so glad to hear this from Jim. In a fog I just walked out the Palliative Care Unit doorway, across the parking lot, and into the Fisher House. After I collected myself I posted this announcement on Facebook:

Facebook Update: Friday 4/26/13, 6:45 p.m.

Our sweet, brave, beautiful son, SrA Bryce Powers left with Jesus today.

I was on his right, holding his right hand. Jim was on his left, holding his left hand. Madison was on the phone, telling him good-bye. He took his last breath at 4:40 p.m. with all three of us saying our good-byes.

Thank you all for standing by our sides for the last six and one-half months. We have felt your prayers, your love, and your care for each of us, and especially for our dear Bryce.

Bryce knew the Lord, believed He died for his sins, and accepted Him in to his heart. Bryce is in a better place!

John 3:16 (NIV)
"For God so loved the world that he gave his one and only Son, that whoever believes in him shall not perish but have eternal life."

We will post the arrangements at a later time.

Love you all!

Love, Cathy

Life Offline

I WILL NEVER FORGET the last day or moments my son breathed on this earth. They call it "transitioning" and "getting ready to pass." We were told there are no absolutes when it comes to the moment of death.

Some say the experience of watching a loved one pass away, although sad, can be beautiful or peaceful. Others describe their loved one in the last seconds of life, saying something like, "They raised their hands in the air, and with eyes wide open and a big, radiant smile, they called out 'Jesus!' as they took their last breath."

None of these things happened with Bryce. It was a slow process of shutting down, a completely tragic physical death unfolded before our eyes. We watched our beautiful son breathe, and then at 4:40 p.m., he took his final breath.

Bryce lived 7,777 full days on this earth; his spirit then returned to God for his next assignment.

Chapter Twenty-Seven

Going Home Alone

We stayed the night at the Fisher House. I slept on and off, feeling like I was in a fog. The next morning, we packed the car, then went back inside to say our good-byes to friends, who now felt more like family. After we checked out of our room, we walked over to the Polytrauma Unit to say good-bye.

We gave and received our last hugs from the amazing men and women who had worked so hard for five months taking care of Bryce and our family. There was pain in many of their faces and also love. I knew they understood and were experiencing some of the huge loss we were feeling. I was thankful for all they had done for Bryce and for our family.

Then, with nothing left to do in Richmond, we began our five-hour car ride home. It was such a strange sad feeling to leave without Bryce. I kept having a sensation come over me that I was forgetting something important. I then reflected on Bryce, faced reality, and knew he would never be able to come home with us. Similar thoughts and emotions played havoc with me, over and over all the way home, replaying the hope and then the pain..

It must be similar to what people experience when they give birth to a stillborn child and they leave the hospital without their baby. They have the car seat, the crib, and all the toys, but no baby. Our car was literally filled with everything from Bryce's hospital stay, but no Bryce. It was such a horrible feeling.

From day one, I took so many pictures and videos, hoping to share them with Bryce. I paid his bills and kept his credit good, all for nothing. We were going home without him.

I couldn't believe he died without me; we were always so close. I couldn't imagine living without him, and now I didn't have a choice. I wasn't able to fix him.

We decided not to tell any of our neighbors we were coming home. We just wanted to get into our house, pull the blinds, and be alone for a while. I didn't want any visitors. I didn't want to hear anyone tell me it was God's will—or even that it was not His will. I didn't want anyone to tell me anything.

I just wanted to see Madison, our Chihuahuas and our cat. I couldn't wait to put on my pajamas, climb into bed, and pull the covers over my head.

I waited until the following day to post this message on Facebook:

Facebook Update: Sunday 4/28/13

Home Sweet Home! It has been a long time. I especially loved the big "dog pile hug" I received from our five Chihuahuas.

Jim, Madison, and I all appreciate your many prayers and words of comfort. Thank you so much! We are working out the final arrangements for Bryce. Hopefully we will be able to post the details midweek. Mother's Day weekend will be the time frame for the local services.

Love, Cathy

Chapter Twenty-Eight

Grieving in Our Own Way

MAY

Facebook Update: Wednesday 5/8/13

Lamentations 3:22-23 (ESV)
"The steadfast love of the LORD never ceases; his mercies never come to an end; they are new every morning; great is your faithfulness."

I sure miss all my prayer warrior friends! Thank you so much for your continued love, prayers, and well wishes during this time. God is good! He is faithfully sustaining us during this extremely difficult season. I will share more about this at a later time.

The amazing Patriot Guard riders are helping us to bring our son home for his visitation and funeral services. What an amazing honor and experience it will be to see Bryce as he arrives back home via US Air on Thursday afternoon. Then he will be escorted and protected by his fellow brothers and sisters all the way back to Monroe, NC. I have heard that as the hearse and the line of Patriot Guard riders and police escorts him, you are welcome to join the flag line along the published route. I think this is so cool!

The Patriot Guard posted this at the end of their Ride Mission invitation:

"Please join us in standing for Bryce; as he stood for us!"

Wow! I know Bryce would just love this! He would love knowing how much people cared about him!

Love, Cathy

Life Offline

The military casualty liaison from Shaw Air Force Base brought all the necessary paperwork for our signatures. All three of us were presented with Gold Star lapel pins, and they expressed their condolences. They explained the procedures for a funeral at Arlington National Cemetery so we could prepare and decide what we wanted written on Bryce's headstone. They explained what they would cover financially, and what our obligations would be. Items like flowers and bagpipers were not included, so we had to make preparations for those extras.

I had received an email from a friend introducing me to the Patriot Guard, a group of patriots who ride their motorcycles to escort the families of fallen veterans. Their mission is to stand with you and stand for your loved one, but they must receive a personal request from the family.

I contacted the North Carolina Patriot Guard and asked them if they would stand for Bryce. They said they would be honored to be at the airport to receive Bryce's body and stand for him at his visitation and funeral. They also promised to contact the Virginia Patriot Guard to stand for him at Arlington.

We were deeply moved by the extraordinary service they provided our family. They worked with police and fire departments escorting Bryce from the Charlotte airport to the funeral home, a twenty-five–mile drive. They had encouraged people to stand along the funeral route holding and waving their flags. Hundreds of caring Americans stood at attention and saluted as we passed by. Many of these fire trucks extended their ladders across intersections with enormous American flags suspended from them. We had a multi-county police escort, with officers at the front and rear of the procession, with dozens of Patriot Guard motorcycle riders escorting Bryce's body, and our family, all the way to Monroe.

Facebook Update: Thursday 5/9/13, 8:00 a.m.

Today the tears won't stop flowing. We get to see our sweet Bryce in a few hours. They are bringing his body home.

The FAA and Charlotte Airport USO have graciously granted us permission to go right out on the tarmac, along with the Honor Guard from Charlotte Air Force Base and troops from Shaw Air Force Base, to welcome him home with honor, love, respect, and open arms. Lord Jesus, please help us be brave and stand tall. I sure miss my sweet, brave son.

I have heard that some people will be standing on the sides of the road as we get closer to McEwen Funeral Home, on Main Street in Monroe, helping to welcome Bryce home with us. Our Red Cross family is also setting up a canteen to help take care of the Patriot Guard riders and law enforcement officers helping to protect

him as they bring him home. We have so much to
be thankful for.

Exodus 15:2 (ESV)
"The LORD is my strength and my song, and he
has become my salvation; this is my God, and I
will praise him, my father's God, and I will
exalt him."

Love, Cathy

Life Offline

When Bryce's body arrived at the Charlotte airport we went out
onto the tarmac to meet him. Everyone was quiet, and all the
passengers were watching out the window of the airplane. We
were joined by a professional photographer named Elmo who
took pictures of all this for our family as a free service.

A group of airmen from Shaw Air Force Base received Bryce's
casket from the airplane. They saluted him and then brought him
down the conveyer belt onto the tarmac where Jim, Madison, and
I were standing. I broke down in uncontrollable sobs when I saw
his casket emerge from the plane. The weight of this huge loss
was just too much to control myself. Jim and Madison both cried
too, but they were silent as the tears streamed down their soaking
wet faces. We all just stood there holding on to and hugging each
other.

It was beautiful to see the respect Bryce was given by his brothers
and sisters in arms. The pilot asked the passengers to remain in
their seats until Bryce's body could be taken off the plane and
received by our family.

This was one of the lowest, most difficult days of my life.

We got into the funeral car with Bryce in the hearse just ahead of us. We followed the police escort and Patriot Guard riders on the long journey to Monroe.

When we arrived at the funeral home, they brought Jim and me into a private room where they opened up Bryce's casket for our first viewing. We were shocked that there were freckles all over his face, and he looked like Howdy Doody. Apparently, the funeral home in Virginia had somehow received a poor quality photo of Bryce, in which he appeared to have freckles, so they airbrushed them on. He looked nothing like he did in real life.

"Oh no, no, no," I said to the funeral director. "This is all wrong. Look at all those freckles."

He looked at me, probably examining the freckles on my face, and he said, "It is?"

"Bryce didn't have any freckles."

"You're kidding!" He pulled out some paperwork, looked it over and pointed, "Two officers signed off on this."

Jim shot right back. "We don't care. He did not have freckles."

"I can change this," the director explained, "but he's not dry yet."

He explained the original makeup had to dry overnight, then he could make adjustments before the public viewing the following day.

Facebook Update: Thursday 5/9/13, 6:30 p.m.

Thank you to the crew and flight attendants on US Air flight 1619, the Patriot Guard riders, the Charlotte USO, the TSA, the Shaw AFB Honor Guard, the Mecklenburg and the Union County sheriffs who kept us all together and safely rolling through the red lights. I also want to thank the police officers, state troopers, and fire departments of all counties and cities between the Charlotte airport and the funeral home in Monroe, who so proudly displayed their huge American flags, blocked intersections, and saluted Bryce as his hearse passed by.

I also want to thank Jay Glazebrooks, Bryce's friend and "USAF Escort" who flew in on orders from Aviano, Italy, to stay with Bryce's body.

Love, Cathy

Facebook Update: Saturday 5/11/13, 2:00 p.m.

Bryce's "Celebration of Life" *service* was at Benton Heights Presbyterian Church, in Monroe, North Carolina.

Life Offline

On the morning of his funeral, we were able to have one final look at Bryce before we went to the church. We said our final good-bye and then they closed the casket and draped it with an American flag.

The Patriot Guard riders escorted us from the funeral home to the church. Once again, we were brought to tears by the multitude of American flags placed by the Patriot Guard riders along the side of the road.

Upon arriving at the church, we were asked to wait in an adjoining room as they wheeled Bryce's coffin into place.

Accompanying us were Gwyn, Tom, and Alice Dailey; my wing sister Marie Stevenson; and representatives from the Red Cross.

Bryce loved the pastor of this church, Rev. Paul Saleeby. He served with him during a Vacation Bible School week before leaving for boot camp. They worked together coordinating sports time in the church gymnasium with the children.

Jim asked Pastor Paul if Bryce's funeral could be held at the church, and he replied, "Oh yes, absolutely! No problem!"

There were several moments that stood out during Bryce's Celebration of Life service. One of them was Pastor Paul reading a quote that we repeated every day in the final days of Bryce's life: "Last breath on Earth, first breath in Heaven."

Throughout the service, the guests could view a slideshow of Bryce's life, including a video of him encouraging fellow cadets and saying good-bye before he left to begin his active duty career.

We were honored to have Sheila Crunkleton, our friend and local director of the American Red Cross, speak at the funeral. She shared how Bryce had volunteered for the Red Cross over the years, as our entire family had in one way or another.

Captain Louis Werder, Bryce's high school Air Force Junior Reserve Officer Training Corps (AFJROTC) Commander, shared how Bryce had remained focused on his goal to join the Air Force. He was proud to be a part of Bryce fulfilling his dream.

Rather than expressing sadness, Madison shared some funny memories about Bryce. She told of how she had picked a touristy foot-long pen on one of our vacations. A few days later, Bryce noticed "#1 Grandpa" on the side of the pen. He laughed hysterically, and that became a family joke for years.

She continued, telling about when Bryce was stationed in South Korea and mailed her a beautiful music box for Christmas, inscribed, "Grandmothers Are Special Blessings." He picked it out as a joke, but he also knew that she collected and cherished music boxes.

She shared another humorous memory with everyone that took place at the Charlotte airport while we waited for him to board his plane to Japan. After our good-byes, we were walking away, and suddenly he went running past us shouting that he was at the wrong gate. Time was now critical so he flagged down a motorized shuttle to get him to the proper gate. We followed on foot. He had to get to the plane before it left without him. We laughed so hard once we knew he was not going to miss his flight. We got to hug and kiss him one more time, and then his plane taxied away.

Little did any of us realize, this was the last happy memory we shared with Bryce as a family.

Jim talked about how amazing it was that Bryce lived only twenty-one years and yet had experienced so much in life. He had achieved all his goals and fulfilled all his dreams. He dreamed of having a father someday. Then Jim adopted him, and he got a Dad who loved him and taught him about life. He dreamed of serving in the Air Force, and he did that with distinction. He dreamed of living in Japan. He dreamed of serving God, and we were so happy to learn that he was still chasing after God until the end. He wanted a cool, little convertible. He had that. He dreamed of going to college to learn computer programming. He had recently enrolled, and it was during his first semester that his accident occurred.

Gwyn's husband, Tom, a retired Master Chief, knelt on one knee and presented me with an American flag. Madison received a flag from Bryce's high school AFJROTC group.

Hearing these stories, watching the videos, receiving the flag, and feeling all of the emotions was bittersweet. The entire afternoon was a blur.

On Mother's Day we drove up to Langley Air Force Base in Virginia and checked in to a hotel. I would never have dreamed that my Mother's Day Sunday would be sandwiched between Bryce's Saturday Celebration of Life service in Monroe and his Monday military memorial service at Langley.

The memorial service was held on base in the beautiful Langley Chapel. The Tudor-Gothic design was built in 1935 of handmade brick, with notable exterior and interior features, including a Celtic cross above the rooftree, a flagstone floor, exposed rafters and beams, and gorgeous stained glass windows.

An officer from the Pentagon read through a list of Bryce's achievements in the military. I was so proud of his service to our country.

I had worked for almost a decade in Virginia Beach, which was not too far away, so many of my former coworkers came to support us. Jim and Madison both gave the same speeches. Then the honor guard presented Madison and me with individual triangular folded American flags. They also gave Madison a beautiful engraved wooden box to hold her flag.

After the service, we went out to dinner with friends and family members. Then we headed back to the hotel, and went to bed early. We were all so exhausted, going through the motions, and not really feeling very much.

We had instructions to meet outside the main gate at Arlington National Cemetery, on Thursday, May 16. Staff members were there to answer our questions and line up our cars for the procession. There were so many cars that they eventually allowed a second row to form. The Patriot Guard lined up in front of us, and we rode behind Bryce's hearse.

The burial was very formal. There were rows of chairs for family under a canopy facing the casket, and everyone else stood. An outstanding military chaplain gave an emotional, personal message. I was presented with the triangular folded flag that had been draped across Bryce's casket. This American flag traveled with him from the time of his passing until now. Madison received an honorary sibling American flag, which was also folded. At that point, the bugler played a moving rendition of Taps. When this was finished, we concluded the service with a lone bagpiper in a kilt playing "Amazing Grace," just as Bryce requested. The entire ceremony was recorded by a professional photographer.

Afterward, there were lots of hugs and shaking hands with military, family, and friends. Before they departed, everyone was given a special gift to remind them of Bryce. The memento I had designed was a black-and-white, hockey puck size foam stress ball, with a design on one side and on the other side the following words in red: "SrA Bryce Powers, January 9, 1992 – April 26, 2013, Final AMMO Call."

Before leaving Arlington, Madison and I each received an engraved wooden triangular, American flag display case to hold and protect our meaningful flags. Jim was presented with a beautiful blue crushed-velvet bag, containing the brass shell casings from the three-volley salute, also known as the twenty-one–gun salute, executed during Bryce's burial ceremony. We were also given a special permit allowing us to drive in to the hallowed grounds when visiting Bryce's gravesite. It was explained to us that driving in the cemetery is only allowed for handicapped visitors and those attending a burial or visiting a private gravesite.

All of a sudden, everything was over.

Chapter Twenty-Nine

Where to Go from Here?

Facebook Update: Wednesday 5/29/13

Dear Prayer Warriors, the last couple of weeks have been extremely hard. The pain is too much, or at least it feels like it is. I miss Bryce! Everything about him! It will take time, prayer, and continued faith to heal my broken heart.

Please, if you will, continue to pray for our family as we daily, and at times minute by minute, choose to trust God for His healing touch.

Thank you again for all your love, prayers, thoughts, and care for Bryce and our family. We are so thankful to each of you!

Love, Cathy

Life Offline

Since his death, I usually go to Arlington by myself to visit Bryce. I know he's not really there, but it's where his body is. For a long time, Jim and Madison didn't come with me. Jim usually says it's because he has to work, and Madison always has a good reason not to join me either. I, on the other hand, want to go pay him a visit every time I get the chance.

Occasionally, I travel alone to places where people in our military family are doing something in Bryce's honor; someone may be running a 5K, a half marathon, or even a full 26.2-mile marathon while wearing Bryce's picture with his name, rank, and birth/death dates on their back. This is such an amazing thing for them to do, and it always makes me so happy to know Bryce is not forgotten and that people still care about him.

We have only traveled to Arlington as a family once since the funeral. I get upset sometimes, because I don't understand why Jim and Madison don't want to go with me.

The psychiatrist at the VA in Virginia told us that everybody heals and deals with grief differently. This is the truth!

Jim and Madison are not the type of people to open up and talk to others about Bryce very often. In complete contrast, I talk to everyone, including strangers, about him whenever I get an opportunity. So I have to keep reminding myself that there is no good and no bad response to Bryce's death.

We all deal with death in different ways, and I just have to accept that the way I grieve is different from the way Jim and Madison are grieving.

Through God's grace, we're all making progress, but we are still grieving—and always will.

JUNE

Thank you so much for thinking about and praying for Jim yesterday on Father's Day. I know our prayers made a huge difference and I'm sure the big juicy roast, potatoes, carrots, and onions I slow-cooked all day, helped a little bit too. Praise God, Jim had a nice relaxing day.

I have not shared much about my thoughts or feelings since Bryce passed away. I have wanted to, but at the end of the day I have pretty much convinced myself that most people, even mighty prayer warriors, might become tired of the roller coaster of emotions I am going through. Yet, here I am, taking a chance, still wanting to keep sharing with you.

First of all, I want to share something about my experience thus far with grief. Please note, I am not an expert in the field or claim to hold any specialized degrees on the subject. I am just sharing my personal "Momma experience" with you.

Grief, for me, has been at times an off the charts physical, emotional, and spiritual pain like I have never known or felt before.

This may seem overly simple to some, especially to all of you that have walked this grief-walk before me, but I was so taken by surprise by the awesome force of pain that hit me, I would like to take a minute to try and explain it.

I always thought grief was a sad feeling people felt when someone they love passes away. For example, when my ninety-six-year-old Grandma died, I felt sad inside. It was an emotional sadness. I loved her, missed her, and thought a lot about the memories we had shared together. However, knowing she had lived such a long, productive life helped ease the sadness and even brought me some comfort. I knew she was finally going to be with Grandpa, her parents, and her many loved ones that had already gone home before her. I was also happy she was able to trade her life here, and living in a rest home, for Heaven.

I now realize, at forty-six years old, how little I actually knew about grief. I have thought about the many friends and acquaintances I have known over the years who have lost someone near and dear to them. Even though I had always felt bad for them, and prayed for them, I had always equated what they were going through to my own experience of my grandmother's passing.

When Bryce was going through the transition process and preparing to leave this world, I literally felt like I was having a heart attack. The physical, emotional, and spiritual pain was by far the worst pain I have ever felt.

It scared me.

I could feel the pain coming, getting stronger, and moving to different areas inside of me. I remember thinking that I was pretty sure I was going to be dying with Bryce. Every once in a while, the pain would feel like invisible hands wrapped around my neck, and I could feel them squeezing tighter and tighter, choking me.

Just when I thought for sure I couldn't take another breath, I would begin to weep uncontrollably. Amazingly, as the tears flowed, the physical, emotional, and spiritual pains would seem to lighten up a little and every once in a while they would almost disappear completely.

Even though I hated going through it initially—and I continue to go through it daily—I believe this entire grieving process is an amazing part of the plan. It's a gift from God, and also a necessity to help my broken heart eventually heal.

My hope and faith remain in the Lord. He knows more than I do about bearing burdens, experiencing pain, and having a bruised and broken heart.

I am comforted by His loving words.

Psalm 34:18 (NIV)
"The Lord is close to the brokenhearted and saves those who are crushed in spirit."

John 16:22 (NIV)
"Now is your time of grief, but I will see you again and you will rejoice, and no one will take away your joy."

Lamentations 3:32-33 (NIV)
"Though he brings grief, he will show compassion, so great is his unfailing love.

For he does not willingly bring affliction or grief to anyone."

And last but not least:

Isaiah 66:13 (NIV)
"As a mother comforts her child, so will I comfort you; and you will be comforted...."

Love, Cathy

JULY

I saw him.

I saw Bryce once when he came to me in a dream. It was a full-circle thing. As soon as I woke up, I ran across the house, bawling, to Madison's room. I woke her up out of a sound sleep, crying, and told her, "Madi, Madi, I saw Bryce and he's okay!" It was like I had come full circle. It was amazing!

Facebook Update: Monday 7/29/13

I realize some may think this update strange, and that's okay. I want to share my experience with you anyway. I hope it helps at least one person as much as it has helped me.

Bryce came to me in a dream on Thursday, July 25, at 8:00 a.m.

I had already been awake for an hour or so, preparing morning coffee and packing lunch, helping Jim get ready for work. After he left, I lay back down in our bed with my iPad to look up a few things on the Internet.

I drifted off to sleep, and that's when I had my very first dream about Bryce since his accident. This is what happened:

All of a sudden, Bryce was standing very close to me, wearing the same shirt he wore in our last family portrait. He was standing on my right. Our heads and faces were very close to each other, and everything seemed perfectly normal, happy, and just like the good old pre-accident days.

He spoke to me, saying something like, "No one better take anything out of my box. That's my box."

He spoke with a half grin and half serious expression on his face. This seemed familiar to me, like he was perfectly healthy and still living at home.

He does have a special box too. He has had it for years and has always kept a lock on it to keep me and Madison out of it. It holds his special coins, keepsakes, and collectibles. I remember thinking in my dream how neat it was, and how thankful I am to be able to dream and see the old healthy Bryce again. It was like I was watching him on TV, and I was seeing an old clip of us together from the past.

Then, all at once everything about my dream changed to the "here and now." Our eyes locked, time seemed to stop, and it seemed like Bryce looked right through me, as he spoke with the most incredible, heartfelt, loving, compassionate, gentle, and yet strength-filled voice. He simply said, "I'm sorry Mom."

In an instant, everything that has transpired since Bryce's accident flashed through my heart and mind. All of my senses exploded with pictures, smells, feelings, and sounds. The accident, the hospitals in Misawa, Okinawa, Hawaii, and Virginia, the doctors, the medical teams, the shared connections, the funerals, the burial. All of it!

I was so overcome with an electrocuting feeling of tingling and emotion, I instantly woke up sobbing.

I immediately called Jim at work to tell him what had just happened. I was both hysterical and happy, wondering aloud if this experience could have been the real deal and if it was really my sweet son letting me know that he was okay. Jim believed it was real, and he gently comforted me until I was able to calm down a bit.

After I hung up with Jim, I ran in to share my experience with Madison. As soon as I told her what Bryce had said to me in my dream, exactly how he said it, and how real it all was, she began sobbing right along with me. I was so glad I had good news to share with Madison this time. I felt bad she was crying, but knowing it was a happy release of tears made it much better this time around.

Nothing like this had ever happened to either of us though, so as the morning progressed, Madison and I started second-guessing whether this sort of encounter could happen. We were going back and forth with our thoughts.

"If Bryce was in Heaven, how could he have spoken to me?" and, "Could all this grief somehow have pushed me over the edge?" I even wondered, "Am I crazy?"

By noon, Madison and I decided it best to call our very kind and compassionate pastor friend to get his thoughts. We wanted to know if this kind of "visitation" is bad, or seemed crazy or even believable? So we called the pastor and requested an emergency meeting. He quickly obliged, and we left to meet with him immediately after hanging up the phone.

Pastor Saleeby listened to everything I had to share, and then comforted both of us by saying that he believes experiences like this do happen. He said that Bryce was somehow allowed to visit and show me that even though he passed away, he is still Bryce, that he is happy, fully healed, whole, and doing well.

Wow! What comforting thoughts for us! I am so thankful to have had this amazing experience with my sweet and extremely missed son! I hope it touches you in a good way too! Thank you for allowing me to share it with you all!

Matthew 5:4 (NIV)
"Blessed are those who mourn, for they will be comforted."

Love, Cathy

Chapter Thirty

The Rest of the Story

AUGUST

Today we received Bryce's autopsy report.

We were able to discuss the findings with Dr. Pai and Dr. Wright. Both experts walked us through the lengthy report, line by line, educating us in layman's terms as we read along to help us better understand all Bryce had been through.

I cannot begin to tell you how relieved I was once I saw on paper, typed out in black and white, just exactly how catastrophic Bryce's brain injuries were. There were many complex layers of cell death, shattered bones, aneurisms, lesions, and holes, caused by both traumatic and nontraumatic injuries.

We finally had definitive evidence that outside of a miracle from God, Bryce would never have regained his functions. The decision to let Bryce pass was the right one. His brain injuries simply could not be fixed by man.

I understand Bryce's death had to come before this autopsy could be performed. But trust me, this was not the way any parent wants to find out they made a good decision and receive answers to some of their once unanswerable questions. Even with the answers in front of us, it was still so painful. The terrible ache in my heart was bearable only because I had laid Bryce before God, faithfully trusting Him to heal him or remove the suffering.

We were told that if we had taken him home, we could have just tilted him to change a diaper and any of those aneurisms could have broken and he would have died instantly. It's dangerous to have even one, and he had hundreds.

He had holes throughout where the brain cells had died, and then were dissolved back into his body. Every one of the experts was shocked that he was able to live as long as he did.

Jim said it perfectly. "Well at least we know. Too bad we had to find it out in this order. It would have been great to have this up front. It would have saved us a lot of grief."

I felt better that at least we knew that God probably wouldn't be mad at us. I had felt so guilty. Jim and Madison would get so upset with me, and say, "STOP!" But my feelings were real. I had been worried that we were in big trouble with God.

According to scientific research, after three months there was a zero percent chance that Bryce would ever wake up. Of course his doctors still tried to help him somehow emerge.

In the end, that's the only thing that gave me peace.

Facebook Update: Wednesday 8/28/13

First and foremost, I would like to say thank you for continuing to pray for our family! I believe your prayers have made, and continue to make, a huge difference in our lives! I thank the Lord for each and every one of you!

I would also like to take a minute and share my grieving Momma's heart with you.

I am determined I will not be crushed by my circumstances! I will keep on loving, trusting, and believing God regardless of the painful feelings and emotions that sometimes seem to overwhelm me.

For those who have not experienced the loss of a child, it's hard for me to put things into words so you can better understand. For me there's a battle raging inside of my heart' a grief war, if you will, being fought in my mind, body, and soul on a daily basis. The horrific and relentless attacks on my whole being are so extremely crushing and fierce at times, that I wish I could have traded my life for his a million times over.

Some days I'm angry and I want to fight the whole world. Some days I want to run away. And some days I want to curl up in a ball and simply give up. These feelings are real and part of the grief war. They sneak up on me when I least expect them. I literally have to fight through these battles one at a time, asking my Heavenly Father to rescue, guide, and strengthen me. He is my Battle Buddy.

I have to continually remind myself my Commander sees everything from beginning to end, while I, the soldier, am only able to see and experience a few tiny clips of my life scenes at a time.

I battle daily to let go of my plans, desires, and dreams. Instead, I grab hold of God's plans. I accept His love, trust in His promises, and try to fully allow Him to be in charge.

This is not easy for me, or a onetime deal! I have to continually hand over the reins to God, surrender my thoughts, my fears, and, of course, my control.

Honestly, I don't always do it! However, I have noticed the more I surrender myself to God, the more comfortable I have become in trusting Him with my life. Amazingly enough, His sweet peace and comfort continue to show up and hug my soul every day.

God has continued to be faithful in healing me, loving me, and leading me closer to Him.

Today, I made it to a place in my heart where I genuinely felt "I don't want to trade His peace for my plans!" I knew this truth in my head already, but today was the first time I felt it inside my heart.

God is so good to me! Another "faith battle" won!

Yes, the battles are rough! With that said, knowing God will never leave me or forsake me, that I will see Bryce again, and that this war has already been won sure makes my life better. I know His Word is completely true when it says:

"I can do all things through Christ who strengthens me!" Philippians 4:13 (NKJV)

Love, Cathy

Deuteronomy 31:6 (NKJV)
"Be strong and of good courage, do not fear nor be afraid of them; for the LORD your God, He is the One who goes with you. He will not leave you nor forsake you."

OCTOBER

This coming weekend will mark the one-year anniversary of the day that instantly changed our son, our family, and each of our lives forever. We are thankful for our military family, our relationships with old and new friends, and also for the many amazing prayer warriors around the world.

Sounds strange probably, but to me it doesn't feel like a year ago. At times, it feels like I just woke up from a long nap and I'm still groggy, trying to fully wake up from this dream, or I should say, nightmare.

In spite of the great sadness and foggy moments, I thank God for never leaving or forsaking us. I thank God for every need He has miraculously metfor every ounce of strength, mercy, and favor He has provided.

For all of you who have continued to care about, love, and pray for our family, I pray He will continue to do a good work in each of your lives, mending each of your broken hearts as we learn to live gracefully with grief.

He is our Healer, our Comforter, and the Provider of Peace!

Love, Cathy

I love and miss you, Bryce Powers!

You are so incredibly missed! I find comfort through our God, knowing I will see your beautiful, smiling face again!

I love you forever, Momma

Chapter Thirty-One

Seventy Days

Nearly ten months after my beautiful and brave son passed away, Jim, Madison, and I were sitting at our kitchen table discussing a book called *Hope Emerges*, by Joseph Macenka. Joe became our friend in Richmond, Virginia, while he was still in the process of writing it. I highly recommend this book because it offers great insight through a behind-the-scenes look inside the lives of patients, their families, and the many heroes taking care of them at the Hunter Holmes McGuire VA Polytrauma Unit.

We gave him permission to follow Bryce and our family as we went through the emerging consciousness program. Joe included some of Bryce's journey in his book.

We were talking about some of the memories and events that had unfolded with Bryce, and I began thinking about the night I clearly heard a male voice say, "I will heal him in seventy days." I told Jim and Madison how sad, hurt, and confused I was still feeling inside. I wholeheartedly believed, with more faith than a mustard seed, and I just didn't understand why Bryce wasn't healed on February 21.

Jim immediately said that I shouldn't feel bad about it. He said my brain probably made it up because I was under so much stress for so many months. "Under so much pressure, you could talk yourself in to almost anything."

I snapped back, "No, that's not right! I know it was real!" Then I started crying. Once again, I was desperate for an answer, praying out loud, begging God to tell me why.

After a while, I got up, went into Bryce's bedroom, and began digging through the boxes that held the physical memories of his last six and a half months of life. As the tears still streamed down my face, I dug until I found the two calendars I had used at the Fisher House and on Bryce's hospital room wall. I brought them to the kitchen table and flipped through the months, seeing all of my daily notes scribbled inside each of the date boxes.

I saw the words "Healing Day" that I had handwritten in December, inside the February 21 date box. I began to feel the emotions, hopes, and memories sweep through my heart again as if it happened yesterday. I closed my eyes, bowed my head, and loudly began crying out to God, asking Him to please give me His wisdom so I could understand why He did not heal Bryce in seventy days.

"I know I heard the voice, and I felt Your peace come over me. I believed it as soon as I heard it. I never doubted You or Your healing power. I knew You would heal Bryce. I just don't understand why it didn't happen."

"Please give me Your wisdom and help me to understand." In that moment, I opened the calendar again and began counting forward from the first day of the accident, October 13, 2012, until I reached day seventy.

"Day seventy" was December 22, 2012, the exact same day Jim watched Bryce's spirit rise up out of his broken body, leaving through the Polytrauma Unit ceiling tiles.

How amazing God is to answer my cry for help! He heard my desperate cries and gave me His wisdom. He helped me to understand and allowed me the opportunity to finally see without a shadow of doubt that He did heal Bryce in seventy days! He just did it in His own perfect way.

Epilogue

Line of Duty

More than seventeen months after Bryce's accident, and more than eleven months after Bryce passed away, we received an email from Jackson with the following quote:

The "Line of Duty" was complete and Bryce was found "In the Line of Duty." … I know that gives you peace. May God continue to guide you and the family. May He also continue to give you peace.

God has certainly sustained each of us, and we realize He is the only reason we continue to move forward in life.

YUKO

Yuko, Bryce's ICU nurse in Japan, has remained a special part of my life. Thanks to modern technology, we have been able to stay in contact through Facebook, emails, and Skype. The close bond between us is supernatural. I say this because Yuko recently shared with me that from the moment we met in Japan, she could understand every word that I spoke in English. She said that Gwyn would speak and she comprehended nothing. Other American "hospital visitors" would speak and again, she understood none of it. Amazingly enough, every time I spoke to her, each of my words would translate effortlessly. It really surprised her when this began. She knew it was a special gift and was shocked by it, but at the same time it drew her to me. She told no one this was happening until two years later when she opened up and shared it with me. She said she convinced herself that I must have known how to speak a universal language through my eyes, face, hands, and personality, and with the love I had inside my heart for my son.

The more I thought about this supernatural language gift, the more convinced I was that God had intended it for a purpose. I wondered if maybe it was to help facilitate good care for Bryce while he was in her ICU. If that were the case, then why was this gift still working more than two years after Bryce had passed?

Feeling such a strong bond to Yuko and wanting Jim and Madison to also have an opportunity to know her like I do, I invited her to come visit us in Monroe for a month. She accepted. In May 2015, Yuko landed at Washington Dulles Airport. I welcomed her to America the best way I knew how—of course, with the red, white, and blue; a yellow smiley-face balloon; and a Starbucks latte. We spent the next few days touring Washington, DC together. We had a great time sightseeing, eating, talking, and shopping. We traveled across the Potomac to pay our respects to Bryce at Arlington National Cemetery twice. The beautiful memories we made are etched into my heart forever.

We eventually made it to Monroe, where Jim and Madison finally got to meet Yuko. We live so far from the city lights that many evenings we brought Yuko outside to watch shooting stars and satellite fly-bys. Thanks to the International Space Station flying overhead and a meteor shower, Yuko thought our enchanted skies were just amazing.

Before the month was over, we drove to Virginia Beach to meet some of my family and to Florida where we enjoyed a magical week at Walt Disney World. We returned home to Monroe for a few days before driving back to Washington, DC. The many hours spent on the road gave us the opportunity to share, explore, and grow closer.

We spent a lot of time talking about Bryce, our individual lives, our hopes and dreams, and even about God. I shared that I didn't think it was only by chance that we met, but instead felt we were supposed to meet. I believe God brought Yuko and me together in this life for a special purpose. Here we live on complete opposite sides of the earth and we speak completely different languages, and yet somehow we became great friends—and she can understand me!

I felt such a desire to keep sharing the love of God with her every chance I could. This had to be the reason God brought us together. It was something I felt very strongly, and I know Yuko felt it too. When I told her how much God loved her and how special she was to Him, she cried because of the strong feelings and the tug she felt in her heart. I explained the salvation plan to her, and on her last day in America, Yuko asked Jesus to come live in her heart.

She confided that her entire life she felt like one of many. She had never experienced the thought that she, as an individual, could be anything special to God until this day.

GWYN

Shortly after arriving in Japan, Gwyn looked me in the eyes and said, "There is nothing you can do or say through this trauma with Bryce that will push me away or make me not love you. I'm extending full grace because I can't imagine this nightmare. I know you, Cathy, because you're my best friend. I know you're a runner. And I just want you to know, you can't run from me, because I'll always be here for you." and she meant every word.

On what would have been Bryce's 24th birthday, I went outside to sit in our gazebo and reflect on his life—and on life without him. As I sat, my eye caught the motion of the wind chime I had purchased with Gwyn in Hawaii, our best friends wind chime.

Immediately, memories of all we had endured together over those months began flooding my heart and mind. I missed her. I missed our friendship.

Sitting alone and finally being honest with myself, I realized she had given all she could to help me in that traumatic season. I knew it all along, but somehow I had run from those truths, and I had replaced them with feelings of anger, jealousy, and blame. I began to put myself in her shoes, and the thought of going through all she did for me was enough to jolt my broken heart. I realized that I would not have wanted to be my friend or go through all that we had endured. I cried out to God, praying for Him to give me the strength to call Gwyn and ask her to forgive me for blocking her out of my life. I was afraid to reach out, and I wondered if it was too late. I worried she would reject me, so I didn't call.

It took me three days to finally build up enough courage to make the call. I was shaking as I dialed her number, sitting a couple feet away from our best friends chime.

Tom answered the phone, and I could tell he was surprised when I said hello and asked for Gwyn. Within seconds, Gwyn took my call. I was out of my comfort zone. I spoke quickly, asking if I could make an appointment with her sometime so that we could talk about all we had been through together, alone and uninterrupted. I told her she might be mad at some of the things I had to say and that if I had the opportunity, I would check us into a hotel for a few days and lock the door until we could discuss everything we'd been through. I continued, saying that I wanted us to have a safe place to kick, scream, cry, laugh, and somehow find forgiveness and healing.

She sort of laughed and said she didn't have the time to go away right now, but that we could talk on the phone. So I set a time for our next phone call, and she accepted.

When I made the second call, we both took turns praying aloud, asking God to give us strength to work through our painful memories and to ultimately help us heal. Then, before getting into the heart of the matter, I thought it best to remind Gwyn of the full grace she promised me from the very beginning of this journey in Japan and that I tend to run away from uncomfortable and painful situations. She remembered her words and said that she still meant them.

The dialogue continued, and we took turns sharing our thoughts and memories and listening to each other. We both agreed this was hands-down, a horrible traumatic experience, and we both had done the best we could at the time. We asked each other for grace and forgiveness in all areas that caused the other pain, and we immediately forgave each other. The healing of our broken hearts, and the restoration of a beautiful friendship, was happening.

At one point in the conversation she was talking and I cut her off mid-sentence, blurting out, "Do you still love me?" She responded, 'Yes," and then giggled. I asked if I had been replaced by a new best friend. She said she does have some good close friends, but that I was still her best friend.

I told her she was still my best friend too.

Incredible! I was so happy it was not too late and that she had not rejected me. We seemed to just pick right back up where we had left off. We talked about our families, our current life situations, and some best-friend innermost-secret thoughts. This healing was real, and I was excited and thankful for a second chance to be best friends with Gwyn.

MADISON

Madison misses her big brother terribly, but her strong faith in God has helped her to stay positive. She is doing very well adjusting to her new normal. She has chosen to deal with her grief by not giving up on life herself. She has worked extremely hard in her studies and community service. She continues to excel by leaps and bounds in her young life.

Her hard work and dedication have certainly paid off. In 2015, Madison was awarded the prestigious Union County, North Carolina, Daughters of the American Revolution (DAR) Good Citizens Award at her high school. She was awarded the Junior Firefighter of the Year Award by the Waxhaw Fire Department, in Union County. She received her high school diploma on May 8, her Associate of Science degree on May 14, and her National EMT Certification on May 21. She also completed her Firefighter Certification in June 2015.

Madison feels she has found her niche and is passionate about helping people as a first responder. She applied for and was accepted at the University of North Carolina at Chapel Hill. She left for college in August 2015. She is working on her bachelor's degree and then plans to further her career in the medical field.

JIM

Jim is now in his thirty-fourth year as a North Carolina unlimited electrical license holder and security professional. The passing of his son has given him the drive to upgrade his skills to the status of instructor and trainer. He now holds a Red Cross instructor certificate to teach lifesaving skills in CPR, First Aid, and automated external defibrillators (AEDs).

In 2015, he received his electrical inspector license for the state of North Carolina and is enjoying his career more than ever.

His grieving is mostly done alone. Instead of sitting and talking about his feelings, he spends time in his woodshop, thinking, creating, and working with his hands. He recently made a one-of-a-kind broadsword-inspired cross in Bryce's memory. Attached to it is a marble plaque inscribed with a photo of Bryce and the words, "This Flag is Raised in Loving Memory of Bryce K. Powers, Age 21, SrA, United States Air Force, January 9, 1992 – April 26, 2013. He Gave His Heart to His Family, His Service To His Country, and His Soul to God." He planted the cross in the ground next to our flagpole in our front yard. This is how he honors Bryce's life and memory, and it's also the best way he's found to work through some of his pain and grief.

ME

I continue to walk this grief journey with both good and bad days. I miss Bryce so much and I don't expect these aching feelings will ever change.

I used to wonder what would become of us if Bryce didn't get better. At times I was sure that this tragedy would swallow our entire family. It is indeed hard to bounce back and thrive with living when faced with such a huge loss. There are times when the grief and pain are so intense, it would be easy to stop living the good life and simply exist instead.

There is nothing anyone can say, do, or promise that will take away the pain one feels when grieving the precious lost life of your child. However, I can say for sure that I am thriving, and I still have a hope and a future promised to me.

What's the secret? The only reason I have made it this far with a smile on my face and joy in my heart is because I'm continually choosing to rely on God to help me through each and every day. He is here in spite of my troubles.

I am confident that he will turn our circumstances, and what was meant to harm or destroy us, into something good.

I believe He helped me write this book to share this message of hope with you. I pray it will be received into the hands of all who need to read it.

The message is simple: God is great, despite what we see, feel, hear, or think. Regardless of the bad things that happen in our lives, if we daily choose to give Him our heart, He will in turn give us His peace. He is the Healer of the wounded and brokenhearted.